WITHDRAWN

BOOKS BY PAUL GOODMAN

Our Visit to Niagara
The Lordly Hudson and Other Poems
The Empire City
The Break-Up of Our Camp
Parents' Day
Stop-Light and Other Noh Plays
The Facts of Life

The Society I Live In Is Mine
The Community of Scholars
Utopian Essays and Practical Proposals
Growing Up Absurd
Drawing the Line
Communitas (with Percival Goodman)
Gestalt Therapy (with F. S. Perls and Ralph Hefferline)
Art and Social Nature
Kafka's Prayer
The Structure of Literature

THE
SOCIETY
I LIVE IN
IS MINE

PAUL GOODMAN

HORIZON PRESS

NEW YORK

To Alice

PREFACE

Here is a collection of angry letters on public morals and politics that I have written in the past few restless years of our society; and I have included with them a few book-reviews and speeches that are very like angry letters.

Two opposite feelings seem to inspire me to write Occasional letters: admiration and indignation. When I admire, however, almost invariably I write personally to those whose article or social work or public stand has moved me. This is too bad, since good people ought to get public praise, and why not from me. But it is as if I consider them, and myself, as a kind of community of the children of light, and the important thing is our mutual acquaintance and love. I have usually found, to my pleasure but not surprise, that our admiration *is* mutual.

But when I am indignant, I air it in public, in order to make clear that "we"—human beings, civilized people, American citizens—cannot tolerate this kind of shenanigans. Even if I write a letter to the offending individual, I tend to send a copy to the press or a responsible official. I don't like the individual, I don't want his acquaintance; but it is as if I want our public environment to maintain at least a minimum standard of common sense and decency, so that we can live and breathe at all. To be sure, the standard is not maintained, but the squawk does me good.

There is another kind of public situation: where I have

a "practical proposal" to remedy a condition that I don't like. In my writing, these constructive suggestions almost always take the form of essays and not letters. They are analytic and didactic. I take it that this is because I do not know or do not trust those in positions of authority, therefore I will not constructively write to them. I try rather to influence the general consensus.

2

In Occasional letters, an author's style and thought are likely to be his sharpest, just as the alivest literary criticism occurs in book-reviews. Here, as in poetry, there is immediate feeling on a concrete issue, and yet there is the objectivity necessary to cope with externally given facts. But though they might be good writing, such letters are likely to be too particular and usually do not add up. In this collection, I have tried to avoid this by arranging these letters in groups that pretty clearly reveal an underlying system of ideas.

I did not write them, however, to reveal a system of ideas, but as outcries. And I print them here as I wrote them. This brings me to why I collect and publish them at all.

They are the squawks of a Citizen. The society in which I live is mine, open to my voice and action, or I do not live there at all. The government, the school board, the church, the university, the world of publishing and communications, are my agencies as a citizen. To the extent that they are *not* my agencies, at least open to my voice and action, I am entirely in revolutionary opposition to them and I think they should be wiped off the slate.

It is appalling how few people regard themselves as citizens, as society-makers, in this existential sense. Rather, people seem to take society as a preestablished machinery of institutions and authorities, and they take themselves as I don't know what, some kind of individuals "in" society, whatever that means. Such a view is dangerous, because it must result in a *few* people being society-makers and exercising power over the rest. Now even if these few —managers, governors, and so forth—were intelligent or had some other excellence, the situation would be disastrous, since a few do not, in sheer quantity, have enough mind, enough attentiveness and concern, to deal with the multifarious problems of society. The result must be, and has been, stupid standardization, stupid neglect, stupid injustice, and a base common denominator of valuation. There is no remedy except large numbers of authentic citizens, alert, concerned, intervening, deciding, on all issues and at all levels.

Another advantage in letters, and the publication of letters, is that they directly confront the individuals responsible for outrage—so far as this can be done in literature at all. By their very form, as well as their occasions, letters name names. Certainly, to name names is essential in our corporate society where there is so much bland anonymity, where activity is thwarted, feeling is debauched, and even death is dealt, and yet no single person can be called to task.

3

I am, as is evident in these letters, a community anarchist. I hold, for instance, that sovereign power must be diminished because it is too dangerous to live with; that people must be free of coercion in order to grow and adventure; that administration should be decentralized as much as possible, in order to multiply sources of initiative and experiment; and that there is a creative and secure-making virtue in face-to-face association in urban and scientific societies. Yet, although an anarchist on principle, I write letters to governors, I serve on a municipal school board, I visit colossal universities, etc. In my opinion, there is no inconsistency.

The institutions that we have are ours and anyway they fill up most of our space. In so far as our predecessors worked and fought for them in the interests of freedom— for the Common Law, the vote, civil liberties, the rule of reason, academic freedom—we have no right to surrender our inheritance to boors and tyrants. It is entailed to us as citizens. And in so far as these institutions offer means and opportunity for free action, I am glad to belong to them or cooperate with them. Naturally, when they become clogs and hindrances, and when their overwhelming drift is in the direction opposite from ours, for instance inevitably toward war, then we cannot cooperate with them or we must actively try to stop them or even to get them out of the way. Generally, as a rule of thumb, my experience has taught me that it is wiser not to abstain or quit, but to cooperate according to one's lights and get fired. This has an excellent effect on others who no longer thought that it was possible to be honest.

P.G.

New York

1

MONEY

•

September 24, 1962

Newton Minow
Federal Communications Commission
Washington, D.C.

Dear Mr. Minow,

I must ask you to call CBS to account for an incident on
their TV broadcast of the opening of Philharmonic Hall
at the Lincoln Center on September 23rd.

The broadcast was sponsored by Corning Glass, and in
the advertisement for that company considerable display
was made of a piece of glass that they had manufactured
as a gift for the Hall. During the intermission, Mrs. Kennedy was maneuvered—whether with her knowledge or
not, I do not know—to stand in front of the same piece of
Corning glass and there be photographed conversing with
Mr. Bernstein, etc.

It is an outrage that the wife of a public servant on the public payroll should be thus exploited to advertise a commercial corporation. I shall have to write to the President to ask him to disclaim responsibility for the incident and to censure the broadcaster. Please advise me of your action.

Sincerely,

cc: John F. Kennedy

[*Mr. Kennedy thanked me for this. Mrs. Kennedy was unaware of the piece of Corning glass. Mr. Minow's office, however, informed me that "the Commission is prohibited from exercising the power of censorship over television networks except in its capacity to license." It therefore advised me to send my objection to CBS and Corning Glass, "since both organizations are interested in objections of the public and do not want to offend if possible."*

I had not asked Mr. Minow to censor but to censure and— blissfully—to revoke the licenses of these networks that have long abused their rights. I certainly have no intention of advancing the Public Relations of CBS and Corning Glass.]

•

September 13, 1962

Editor, *The New York Times*

Dear Sir,

I am fascinated by the logic of the rebuttal by the chemical industry and the Department of Agriculture of Rachel Carson's attack on the pesticides. The chemists argue that if the market slackens because of public alarm, the industry will not want to spend large sums on research. Dr. Harris of the Department of Agriculture, on the other hand, concedes that it is conceivable that a major part of pest control can be achieved by biological means, by balance of nature, but "this is a long way off." Presumably, what

Miss Carson wants is precisely to put the research-money into the safer and better solution and bring it nearer to realization.

The chemists are unfortunately advancing a self-proving hypothesis. The more brains and money are devoted to the pesticides, the more inevitable it will become that no more natural means can be adequate. It will be too late; in some areas it is already too late. And also, if that market continues to be encouraged, there will inevitably be less money and brains available for the better "conceivable" solution. Then it will be blandly stated that there is no better solution, even conceivable.

Yours,

[*This was printed in the* Times *on Sept. 21, 1962.*]

•

March 6, 1960

Associated Students of the University of California

Sirs:

Forgive me if, as a visitor to the University, I make a friendly complaint. Last week I went to the U. Cal.-S.F. State baseball game and I was astounded, and disgusted, to hear over the speaker-system at the end of the 3rd inning a commercial plug for a gasoline company (Tydol). This was quite out of place and soured a pleasant afternoon.

I am not from this state or, as a taxpayer, I should strenuously object to the Governor about using a publicly paid-for setting for such promotion of a private corporation. But more generally, and more important, it is an insult to ingenuous young men, playing for the sport, and to those who come to watch, to associate them with this kind of venal yawping.

I understand that the oil company paid for the PA system. This was generous of them and should have been acknowledged with a grateful note. But the beauty of disinterested patronage is destroyed by their wanting something in return, and especially something as foul as this. Let me urge you to remedy the matter at once.

Sincerely yours,

cc: Governor Brown

[*Governor Brown answered that he would look into it—I do not know with what result. I do not know if this practice was discontinued. The Student Association did not acknowledge my letter. In general at the colleges, the dominant majority of the students is as conformist as the Administration and more lacking in manners.*]

•

December 12, 1959

President of the Board of Education
New York City

Dear Dr. Silver,

At Junior High School 3, and presumably at other schools, the class time has on several occasions been taken up with the use of a rag called *The Educational ABC's of Industry,* a collection of commercial advertisements interlarded with reading matter. Last week my boy and his classmates were required to copy out such literature as

> *C stands for Orange-*Crush.
> *Taste it and see*
> *Why boys and girls are saying,*
> *"Orange-*Crush *for me."*

> *F is for Ford Motor Company*
> *Where the first car grew*

> *To a leading industry*
> *With adventure for YOU.*

> *S is for Sweets, which are made of the very*
> *Best energy products of orchard and dairy;*
> *Of fruits, milk, and nuts, all yummy-delicious*
> *With Protein and Energy, tummy-nutritious.*
> > (National Confectioners' Association)

Allow me to protest the entry of such garbage into the classrooms at all, not to speak of wasting on it time that could better be given to honest and noble writing. Are these the habits of motivation and style that we want our children to acquire? The public school system is not the place to provide training in the use of brand-names. We are just now witnessing exposure of dishonorable commercial practice in TV. It is certainly far worse to subject to it captive children in public schools. Must we again wait for a Congressional investigation?

My son has also put into my hands nearly two dozen brochures distributed in his classes, put out by great semi-monopolies, trade-associations, or princes of Madison Avenue like Westinghouse, Con Edison, Bell, Ford, the National Dairy Council, and Merrill Lynch. These are, of course, more discreetly concocted than the crude brand plugs; but they all the more insidiously turn our public schools into apprentice-training-grounds for such firms. May I urge you to protect our children henceforth from these techniques of "public relations"?

> Sincerely,

cc: Commissioner Allen
  The New York Times

[*The Principal of J.H.S. 3 called my son down to ask why his father had gone over his head to the Board. My son guessed that it might be because I wanted the things out of the whole system, not only one school. "If that's your attitude," said the*

*Principal, "there's no use in talking to you." My son was then
12.*

*Mr. Loretan, the Associate Superintendent in charge of these
schools, wrote me that the material I had quoted was indeed
rather low-grade. And indeed, immediately, all the material
complained of vanished from J.H.S. 3.*

*However, three years later, I find on my visits as a member
of a local school board that similar material has returned.
E.g., at P.S. 165, the* Junior Scholastic, *a weekly that is distributed free and used in an enriched-program class, contains
a sickening cartoon-strip of Bell Telephone, ending, "Next
time you visit us, Chip, I'll show you exciting communications
developments which will be used in the more distant future."
"I'd say the exciting world of future communications has already begun—at the Bell System."*

*Eternal vigilance, etc. I have put the matter on our School
Board agenda.]*

•

March 26, 1961

Editor, *New York Herald Tribune*

Dear Sir,

   In today's homily on Confident Living, Dr. Norman Vincent Peale cites the example of a branch manager called
on the carpet by the firm for having "got involved with
one of the salesgirls." The happy outcome is that after sincere repentance he is transferred to another branch. It es-
capes me what business it was of the firm's in the first place.
Does Dr. Peale really assume that a man who works for an
organization has also consigned to it his body and morals?

Yours,

   [*This one was not printed.*]

•

August 16, 1962

Mr. Geoffrey R. Simmonds
Simmonds Precision Products
Vergennes, Va.

Dear Geoffrey Simmonds,

I am deeply in agreement with your statement made at the Young Executives Conference and quoted in last Sunday's *New York Times* (Aug. 12) "If a person does not take satisfaction in his job, he is sinning against himself by working at it." This is a principal theme in my *Growing Up Absurd* and I use almost identical language in my forthcoming *Drawing the Line*. Indeed, I do not think real democracy is possible except on this principle.

Do you have any suggestions how to implement this principle for the men working in your various plants, more particularly at the "semi-skilled" tasks? My purpose in asking is to try to devise some kind of general program to this effect and try to get the various labor-unions to add this concept to their demands, made specific for various situations. In my opinion, this would very often involve very important changes—certainly in processes, possibly even in products, in training and apprenticeship, and perhaps even in the relations of labor and management. What do you think?

Sincerely,

cc: Eli Cohen, National Committee on Employment of Youth

[*I wrote this one just as fun-and-games. Unfortunately, through an error in addressing, it never reached Mr. Simmonds. Eli Cohen, who wears out his life trying to get jobs for the 65-75% of unemployed urban youth, and worrying about the poor quality of the jobs they do get, was as fascinated as myself as to what the President of the Young Executives would say.*]

•

*[Worley, an admired teacher, refused to prepare some un-
necessary lesson-plans and was fired.]*

December 12, 1959

Commissioner of Education
Albany, N.Y.

Dear Dr. Allen,

I am told that the case of James Worley of Croton Falls
has come to you for review. Allow me to say something on
his behalf.

In content his original protesting action seems to me
beyond doubt correct. I myself have taught every age from
ten-year-olds through Ph.D. candidates and older adults;
it has been my universal experience that formal preparation of a lesson-plan beyond the next hour or two is not
only unrealistic but can be positively harmful and rigidi-
fying, for it interferes with the main thing: the teaching-
contact between the teacher and his class. Worley's disagreement with the administrative order is, to me, simply
presumptive evidence that he is a good teacher and knows
what the right teaching relation is. A teacher who would
seriously comply with the order would likely be a poor
teacher. (Our model must always be the Socratic dialogue,
for the aim is *not* to convey some information but to get
across the information as part of the student's nature and
second-nature, so he can make an individual and creative
use of it.) On the other hand, if the compliance is not serious it is a waste of time, and, as you know, teachers are
burdened with paper-work, much of which is absolutely
necessary.

In form, his protest was certainly insubordinate. But
obviously each of us has the moral and social duty to draw
the line somewhere against obedience to error; and I must
affirm that Worley has drawn it at a very correct place,

namely where the order interferes with the right performance of the job. In the end this is the most sacred and final
obligation of every professional, to do the *work* and to defend the conditions under which the work can be done
well.

I am taking the trouble of writing to you because I think
the issue is of immense importance. Our country is being
systematically emasculated by a sickening waste of human
resources. The efforts of a Dr. Conant to salvage some scientific talent are ludicrously inadequate to the main problem, which is precisely the difficulties created by our social
relations, that keep the inventor from his materials, the
workman from honest labor, the teacher from his students
and subject-matter, and the artist from his public. We
cannot throw away good teachers to save face for mistaken
administrators; it is the glory of good administration precisely to smooth the path for objective work to proceed.
Therefore I urge you to intervene in this case and rein-
state Mr. Worley.

Sincerely,

[*Worley's appeal was denied. Commissioner Allen informed
me that, although there was much right on Worley's side, he
ought to have gone through the proper channels—a procedure
which might have taken several years.*

*On another occasion, the Commissioner pointed out that
Worley had failed the students as a teacher because he had
not shown how to "handle constructively their problems of
adjustment to authority." Worley used, in fact, to teach Tho-
reau in his classes.*]

•

July 17, 1960

Dear Adlai Stevenson,

Arthur Krock, in today's *Times,* has the sentence, ". . .
though the floor demonstration for Stevenson (at the Dem-

ocratic Convention) was very loud, *lavishly financed*, largely sincere, and a masterly Hollywood production, etc." Is the underlined idea reasonably accurate? I am not thinking of paying for the kids' bus-fare or anything like that. If it is accurate, I understand that this is the nature of the ballyhoo-beast.

If it is not reasonably accurate, however, it is absolutely essential that you ask for some kind of apology and make a fairly particular account. It is essential not for your reputation, which does not rest on this specific kind of issue, but because we must begin to cross and deny at every significant point the attitude glibly assumed by Krock. This is considerably more important for our country in the next few years than being President. As you know.

It is my sense, as a writer and artist, that there is a deep and almost universal disgust in the Americans for the system that allows organization and front to nullify skill, inventiveness, and human excellence. What is needed, in order to make it loudly vocal and effective, is no longer demonstration or polemic—the case has been proved—but exemplars, bearing witness. We hoped that you would be nominated by your party; but there is no doubt that you can be far more useful to us as one who stands up, and stands out, as a public figure who is nevertheless a man.

Sincerely,

cc: Eleanor Roosevelt

[*Mr. Stevenson's law partner answered me that Mr. Krock was in error, but that one cannot pursue every such matter.*

Mr. Stevenson's subsequent career has not seemed to me exemplary.]

•

[*My brother, two other Columbia professors, and myself were invited to make an hour's tape for the Columbia student*

radio, WKCR. This was, as we did not know, a program spon-
sored by the Public Relations of the University. My brother
and Professor Robbins chose to discuss, without undue admira-
tion, the new architecture at Columbia; and this portion of the
tape was withheld from broadcast. I demurred and received a
friendly letter of explanation from William Wood, the Uni-
versity's Director of Radio and Television. I then sent him
the following, which, with his letter, managed to get into the
Columbia Spectator, *the student press, which decried the "Cen-*
sorship."]

March 14, 1961

Dear Mr. Wood:

Thanks for your excessively favorable estimate of our
labors on the program "Columbia Today." We did not
intend to cause you any difficulties but merely wanted to
say our say to the radio public and incidentally to help
out a public-service enterprise. May I personally express
my wonder, however, at some of your explanations.

I find simply fascinating your proposition: "Participants
should speak their minds on any subject . . . excepting
controversial topics concerning Columbia." Will you try
to imagine approaching a prospective speaker with this
proposition? How would you phrase it? And supposing he
accepted such an odd condition, what would be his behavior? Before the microphone he might suddenly balk and
exclaim, "My thoughts are supposed to flow freely, but
they have stopped dead at a certain pink elephant whose
name, however, I have agreed not to mention!"

Before we made those tapes, we specifically asked Mrs.
Rathaus if there would be any editing of content—since
some of us have had bad experiences in that line. On a
commercial station we should have insisted on going on
live, to prevent distortion and monkey-business. But she
absolutely reassured us. Now it seems to us that simply as
a point of honor your station would *have* to fulfill a pledge

of your responsible agent. But perhaps we belong to the old school.

However, the two of us who were the most involved, Profs. Herbert Robbins and Percival Goodman, would be glad to discuss the Arts Center with persons "from the Administration present to speak for the defense." Will you set it up, or shall I try to arrange it for them at WBAI?

One last, somewhat legalistic, point. I can understand running a public service station to enhance the public relations of a corporation; but is it not legally rather dubious to *censor* a public-service program in the interest of protecting endowments? Does not that make the station a profit-producing, or at least a profit-protecting enterprise? But more important, I myself do not at all like to think that I am being used "deliberately to give the University a favorable image in its community." I find it vaguely insulting.

Sincerely,

[*The student station was not satisfied. It demanded to air the banned tapes. The President's office then faithfully promised to release them, after they were "cleared of libelous passages." I doubt that there were libelous passages. A long time has now passed, and no such tapes have been released, although both station and the* Spectator *several times have asked for the promise to be kept.*]

•

[*I received a form letter from Ernest Callenbach, the editor of* Film Quarterly, *a new magazine put out by the University of California Press, asking me to contribute "serious articles," since "you are one of the people we count on for good material. We need it badly." I was offended by both the tone and format of the request and answered as follows, receiving no answer in return.*]

1958?

Dear Callenbach,

Just soberly look at the style and format of your "Somewhat confidential memorandum": is that the way to address a serious writer?

It does not seem to occur to you that one reason for your ill-success in getting worthwhile material is the petulant tone with which you ask for it, and the standard that we see writ large. I hear no word of dedication to the art of film, or despair about the present state. All your busy Madison-Ave. rhetoric ("rustling through our in-basket") makes one see nothing but a self-centered concern made worse by editorial posing that has nothing to do with editing, but a good deal with commercial journalism. "We think that *FQ* is an exciting enterprise"—but excitement as such is not an interesting goal. Excitement toward what objective excellence? How am I a member of a team?

To put this another way: when you criticize the style and length of the pieces you reject, I doubt, from your example, that you'd know good writing if you saw it, or that you'd realize that an argument is as long as it's long, no matter what your "editorial" package-preconceptions may be.

"The horse-leech hath two daughters: Give! give!" So says the Book of Proverbs. Why should I? Ask yourself how you persuade me. My guess is that you aspire to the elevation of, say, *Esquire:* but you must remember that *Esquire* persuades us by 20 cents a word. If I gladly contribute to *Dissent, Liberation,* or many a little magazine that comes to me with ingenuous enthusiasm, it is that I ought, noblesse oblige, to serve the public and praise God. But your appeals don't move me at all, at all.

Send me your back issues and let me see. Don't, *don't* send me form letters.

Sincerely,

●

August 28, 1962
Editor, *Columbia University Forum*

Dear Sir:

I must object to a line of argument in Dennis Wrong's pious essay on Max Weber in your summer issue. When Weber is accused of underestimating the clogging of initiative and the bloated overhead of bureaucracies, Wrong says this is "irrelevant. . . . The point remains that most of the activities of bureaucracies today could not under modern conditions even be carried out badly by non-bureaucratic organizations." But in principle, if inefficiencies tend to accumulate, there could be a point at which they outweigh efficiencies; and neverthless the bureaucracies will expand, perpetuate and solidify themselves. And empirically, my rough judgment is that the point of inefficiency could be shown to be already far exceeded in many areas, certainly in urbanism, communications, education, much industrial production, and much trade in commodities, *if the total social labor is taken into account and if the standard of living is criticized.*

The bother is that the style of bureaucracy itself hampers such empirical investigation. It usurps the field and dictates research; its "narrow criteria of efficient performance" are indeed narrow; its departmentalizing defeats a holistic approach; its method of cash-bookkeeping speciously prejudges some of the most essential costs and gains by disregarding them. Bureaucracy itself is a crucial factor in the "modern conditions," and indeed, Professor Wrong's easy-going assumption that our technology, population, etc. "could not be" organized otherwise is precisely the nothing-can-be-done attitude of bureaucracy.

Weber understood that rationalization is a moral and religious style, and a rather lifeless one; nevertheless he

was deeply hypnotized by it—his politics never tran-
scended it. *Therefore* he lays undue emphasis on its polar
opposite, charisma. (It is grim how his disciple, C. Wright
Mills, forgot that rationalization was a style at all, and began to think of it as the nature of things, and so conceived
his fantastic admiration for concentrated "decision-making.") But Weber is wrong, the charismatic leader is not
ethically "neutral." In extreme degrees, both rationalization and charisma are base, unworthy of human communities. They are wasteful of man and resources; they are
slavish and superstitious; they diminish the quality of life;
they stand in the way of the spirit. It is the course of a
reasonable (practical) sociology at present to de-energize
any such polarity.

Yours,

[*Printed in the Fall, 1962 issue.*]

•

[*When I was appointed to local School Board 6 and 8—the
West Side in Manhattan*—The Morningsider, *an Upper West
Side paper, asked me for a statement, printed on September 27,
1962.*]

When I join a local school board in our big system, I
want to be effective, to remedy abuses that can be remedied, to propose new functions that are realistically feasible. Yet among the pressures and limitations of such a
situation, I hope I can retain the philosophic attitude that
asks: what is it all about? is it good? Maybe I make the following remarks to bolster my courage.

Schooling is a natural community function. But our
system is, of course, a complicated artifact and it is compulsory. In such a case, the burden lies on the schools of
continually proving that they are good on the whole, that

they do not do more harm than good. Consider a simple problem: 20 is probably a good class size; but this number is financially "out of the question," so we have 35-40. Is this better than nothing? No, usually it is positively damaging—it turns the children into integers and mechanizes the teacher; and to subject children to what is damaging is evil, even if it is "necessary." Let me be frank. I do not think our schools are good; they cannot be, regimented to a society that is base, venal, and violent, and that puts its wealth into the wrong things. Also, our system developed under older conditions; it has vastly expanded and become a fixture; yet except by a few progressive educators, it is never subjected to profound questioning. But perhaps some, perhaps many, perhaps most children would be better off without the schools we have, even if they then had no schooling at all; except that for many children the home and urban environment is even worse, and for almost all children there is no future, either in learning or in making a living, but by submitting to the unquestioned pattern of these schools.

The drop-outs (at 16) are importantly the victims of poverty, cultural deprivation, race prejudice, emotional troubles; and our sociologists tend to dwell on these background conditions. But if the schools are useless or damaging, the drop-outs are in the right. Their mistake is that they are imprudent, since they diminish their future chances of a decent living. But then the reasonable social policy would be not to try to keep them in school, unless the school is radically changed, but to provide them opportunity for a decent future in some other way. Our society at present can't and won't do this. And by and large, the concern for the drop-outs is because they are a nuisance and a threat, who can't be socialized by the existing machinery.

Numerically far more important than these overt drop-

outs are the children who conform to the schooling (6 to
16 or 20), but drop out internally, daydreaming, their days
wasted, their liberty caged and scheduled, inhibiting their
desires, losing imagination and aspiration. To say it bru-
tally, it is in the schools and from the mass media, more
than at home or from their friends, that the mass of our
citizens learn that life is inevitably routine and phony, de-
personalized, venally graded and bureaucratized; that it is
best to toe the mark and shut up; that there is no place for
spontaneity, simple sexuality, and free spirit. Trained in
the schools, they go on to the same quality of jobs, culture,
politics.

The question "For what Good?" can probe very dras-
tically. For instance, there is a vast anxiety about teaching
reading. And, indeed, reading deficiency is an accumulat-
ing disadvantage that results in painful inferiority, truancy, and drop-out. By the standards of school and the
kinds of success and status that schooling leads to, reading
is crucial. Yet there is something phony here. What does
"reading" mean today? We cannot say that, as humanities
or science, the reading-matter of the great majority is in
any way superior to the movies or TV that the illiterate
can share. Certainly many people would be better off
without most of this mass culture, including the reading-
matter. And why should most people *bother* to learn to
read seriously? In the decision-making of our society, serious literacy is of no practical importance whatever; it is
as powerless as it is rare; and, anyway, those who achieve
it do not do so by the route of "Run, Spot, Run" to *Silas
Marner,* but by their own explorations. It is claimed that
without universal literacy our economy and technology
could not operate. I doubt that this is true for many un-
skilled and many craft and mechanical jobs; and unlike
the expanding industrialism of the 19th century that expanded our compulsory education, or the present situation

in the underdeveloped regions of Africa, Asia, and Latin America, the automated future we face in the United States will have no need for all workers. Rather, in my opinion, it is the kind of urbanism, politics, and buying and selling and other money arrangements that we have, that put a premium on literacy; in my opinion, these are of dubious human value. *In the present dispensation,* we would be as well off if it were socially acceptable for large numbers not to read. It would be harder to regiment people. There would be more folk-culture. Serious letters would benefit if less swamped by trash, lies, and bland verbiage. Much suffering of inferiority would be obviated. And, conceivably, more people might become genuinely literate if it were understood that reading is a useful art with a proper subject-matter, imagination and truth. (Needless to say, my purpose in these remarks is to change the dispensation, so that it will be worthwhile for everybody to read.)

As a loyal academic, I must make a further observation. Mainly to provide apprentices for the war department and the big corporations, there is at present a strong pressure to gear the "better" elementary schools to the colleges and universities. This is the great current reform. But what if the top of the ladder is corrupt and corrupts the lower grades? On visits to 50 colleges everywhere in the country, I have been appalled at how rarely the subjects are studied in a right academic spirit, for their truth and beauty and as part of humane international culture. Rather, the students seek and are given a narrow expertise aimed at licenses and salary, and they are indoctrinated with a national thoughtlessness that is not even chauvinistic. Administrators sacrifice the community of scholars to aggrandizement and subsidized research. Conversely, there is almost never conveyed the spirit that learning is a truly practical, enlightening experience, initiating and giving courage for change, reforming politics, deepening personal and social peace. On the contrary, there is a professional cynicism and the resigned conviction that Nothing Can Be Done. If this is the University, how can we hope for aspiring scholarship in the elementary schools? Everything will be grading, conformist "citizenship," and getting ahead not in the subject but on the ladder. The improvement of "academic" standards is a sell and the bright boys and girls are being had. Some of them know it and balk.

In these circumstances, there is no alternative but that our school system must, from the bottom to the top be open to radical experimentation, to find out how to make itself a worthwhile experience for the children, and to be a seedbed for a better American generation. And there are pernicious influences in the schools, of the corporations, real estate, the military, and police and church, that must be eradicated. Unfortunately, in the nature of the case, a great public system will resist radical experimentation and it will cower before powerful interests. It is with this outlook that I join my local school board.

[*In this same issue of* The Morningsider *appeared the following remarks by Edward Gottlieb, the principal of Public School 165, in District 8: "I would so much hope that the growth of the individual spirit takes place in school and class. Unfortunately, it is more often inhibited, or worse, prohibited. . . . The growth that children do experience in school is due mostly to the presence of other children. They grow more in spite of the teacher than they do because of him."*

It is rather hilarious, and also greatly to our honor, that a member of the School Board and the Principal of a school can say that the schools do more harm than good.]

•

[The Morningsider, *October 18, 1962.*]

Let me follow up my last remarks on the compulsory school system (*Morningsider,* Sept. 27) with a few more "philosophical" reflections.

First, there are ways in which big school systems have nothing to do with education at all. The New York system turns over $700 million annually. It is a vast vested interest and it is very probable that, like much of our economy and most of our political structure (of which the public schools are a part), it goes on for its own sake. In doing so, it keeps thousands busy, preempts the time and space in which something else could be going on, etc. It is also a gigantic pork-barrel for textbook manufacturers and building contractors.

Further, its fundamental design is ancient, yet has not been altered, although its present operation is altogether different in scale and therefore must be in meaning. E.g. (figures of the Board of Education), in 1900, high school graduates were 6 percent of the 17-year-olds, and of the 6 percent, 4 percent went to college. In 1961, nearly 60 percent are graduates, and of these nearly 60 percent are bound for something called college. Likewise, there is a difference between a few hours' attendance in school intermitted in life on a farm or in a city with plenty of small jobs, and schooling that is, essentially, a child's *only* adult contact, apart from family. Thus, a perhaps outmoded institution has become almost the only available way of growing up!

This pre-empting has occurred not only in extent but in intensity. Just as our American society as a whole is more and more tightly organized, so its school system is more and more regimented as part of that organization, with little leeway of its own. In the organizational plan, the schools play a non-educational and an educational role.

The non-educational role is very important. In the tender grades, the schools are a babysitting service, "to relieve the home," in a climate of collapse of the old type of family and of extraordinary neighborhood mobility. In the junior-high and high school grades, they are an arm of the police, providing auxiliary cops and concentration camps unfairly allocated in the budget to the Board of Education. The educational role, as I have said previously, is increasingly to provide apprentice-training for corporations and the war department and to train the young, as Commissioner James Allen has said, "to handle constructively their problems of adjustment to authority."

There is no doubt that the school system has been, and continues to be, a powerful force for the democratizing of our great and mixed population. But we must be careful to keep reassessing it when it becomes a universal trap, and democracy begins to look like regimentation.

This is not the place for a long list of practical proposals to make the schools worth attending for those who are compelled to. But let me offer a few simple ideas toward loosening the Trap that we have been considering. I would suggest the following experiments:

1. Have "no school at all" for a few classes. These children should be selected from tolerable, though not necessarily cultured, homes. They should be numerous and neighborly enough to be a peer-society for one another. Will they learn the rudiments anyway? The experiment could not harm them, since there is evidence (from Sloan Wayland of Teachers College) that normal children can make up the first six or seven years with a few months' good intensive teaching.

2. Largely dispense with the school building for a few classes and use the city itself as a school—the streets, cafeterias, stores, movies, museums, parks, factories. Such a

class should probably not exceed 10 for one pedagogue. The idea is an Athenian one, but is not dissimilar to youth gang work, but not with delinquents and with no need to play to the gang ideology.

3. Along the same lines, but both outside and inside the school building, use the adults of the community who know something or have some other attractive virtue to be the proper educators of the young into the grown-up world: the druggist, the storekeeper, the mechanic, so as to overcome the separation of the young from the grown-up world in our urban life, and to diminish the omnivorous authority of schoolteachers and school buildings. This experience would be useful and animating for the whole community.

4. Make class attendance not compulsory (A. S. Neill). If the teachers are good and the subjects worthwhile, this should soon eliminate absence. The justified reason for the compulsory law is to get the children from the parents, but it must not serve as a trap for the children. A modification might be permission to spend a week or month in any other worthwhile enterprise or environment (Frank Brown).

5. Decentralize the school into small units of perhaps a hundred, in clubhouses combining play, social activity, discussion, formal teaching. Special events could bring together the many small units to a common auditorium or gymnasium so as to give participation in the greater community.

6. For a couple of months of the school year, send children, by twos or threes, to a family-farm to take part in farm life. This would serve to give the farmer cash, as part of the generally desirable attempt to lower the urban-rural ratio, which is now entirely too high.

Above all, apply these or any other proposals to particular individuals or small groups, without the obligation of uniform treatment for all. There is a case for uniform standards of achievement, but they cannot be reached by uniform techniques. The claim that standardization of procedure is more efficient, less costly, or alone administratively practical, is usually false. Particular inventiveness requires thought, but thought does not cost money. And the more the authority to initiate (including the right to make mistakes) is delegated to many, the wiser and freer we shall all be.

●

[*Rose Franzblau writes a regular column of advice on family and emotional problems in the* New York Post.]

October 29, 1962

Editor, *New York Post*

Dear Sir,

Mrs. Franzblau's immediate recourse to deep psychology in the case of the bright little girl who day dreams in school (October 25) is rather astonishing. As one who was a bright child myself and am now a member of the School Board, may I remind her that the schools we have, with their dull curriculum, overcrowded classes, and overworked teachers, are often not good enough to win and keep the attention of lively young minds. If some drop out by daydreaming and some drop out by truancy, the fault is not necessarily the child's.

Sincerely,

[*This was not printed.*]

●

[*In* Dissent, *Summer, 1962.*]

FORMAT AND ANXIETY

[*The following little reportage was commissioned by* Show
*magazine. The editor, Robert Wool, read it in my presence,
occasionally smiling, and he said, "Yes, of course, that's just
how it is." He suggested a few small changes, which were im-
provements; sent the transcript down to be processed for publication; and in due course sent me a check. In a few weeks,
however, he phoned me and told me apologetically that Huntington Hartford, the publisher of the magazine, had absolutely
vetoed the essay, and he returned it to me.*

*This pattern has begun to happen to me frequently, that
work of mine is commissioned, accepted, and paid for by the
working editors, but is vetoed by the "decision makers." I need
not point out to the readers of* Dissent *that it is by such means
that our society presents us with its dull and dangerous mono-
lith. I have also had to withdraw articles in a rage because
the editors of magazines with large circulation have asked me
to delete or tone down accurate pointed references. I have no
doubt that many essays appear, signed by fine writers, that
have been emasculated in this way. May I urge my fellow-
writers to publicize all such incidents, so that the critical intellect can do its job? If we do not band together on this, we
are ruined. The* Nation *would be an appropriate vehicle for
this kind of news.*]

I don't much look at the movies, television, or the other
popular arts covered by *Show* magazine. About once a year
my wife and I go to a movie to see what that is like. Occasionally, if I am immured alone with a TV set, I switch
it on.

Last fall I was at a hotel in Galesburg, Illinois, where
I was to give a speech at Knox College, and I switched on
the TV before going to bed. It was Jack Paar, of whom I
had heard; and his guest was Max Lerner, the historian

and journalist. What I saw astonished and enraged me. Max is, in my opinion, wrong-headed and boring, but he is (sentimentally) earnest; yet he was treated by Paar and *the format of the show* with a disregard bordering on contempt. At one point Max, obviously disturbed, was discussing the necessity of forgiving Germany because of the needs of the Cold War, when suddenly Paar cut him off to hold up a silk stocking and make a pitch. Interrupted, Max made a pitiable face and my heart went out to him. This recalled to me many previous moments of disgust and indignation when we would be listening to terrible radio reports about the invasion of Hungary or a crisis in the United Nations, and they would be interrupted by a jingling commercial beneath the dignity of a grown man to write or speak. How in such a case can the Americans make sense of the news, follow a train of thought, or indeed retain any notion of the reality of the world? . . . Jack Paar switched to a gentleman who did card tricks, and I switched off the set.

Next morning, putting aside my notes, I described to the community at Knox the Jack Paar show of the night before, which some of them had watched. To my surprise this had an extraordinary effect. Many were as if stunned. And in subsequent conversations I came to realize, what would never have occurred to me, that most people do not notice the actuality, what is really present, on their TV screens. They simply go along with the formats that stop thought and prevent feeling. They take the baseness and absurdity of the human figures for granted, and cease to notice them. This explains the puzzling double standard that obtains, how ordinary intelligent people are not overcome by rage and nausea. The audience is not *there* in any present or esthetic way. They are perhaps carrying on an unconscious revery; or they are being sketchily reminded of the various symbols of American society and reliving their own psychosexual pathology (this is Parker Tyler's theory of the movies). The more sophisticated, accepting the format and the devaluation of persons implied in it, discuss whether it is well or poorly done for what it is. This is the usual hip criticism of "popular culture." Obviously, such responses are disastrous to any use of this serviceable medium as communication, or to this audience ever having a thoughtful or artistic experience. (In an artwork there is no extrinsic format and less and less is taken for granted.) If this is indeed the general situation with the audience, I am afraid that the whole enterprise had better be discontinued: it is our duty to boycott and destroy it.

I have had occasion to experience how the format stops thought and feeling also for the persons in the program. I am often on the radio and sometimes on TV, for these have a wide audience that I like to reach. But it is hard to retain one's identity. At best there is an unpleasant battle in the studio. An interviewer asks me a question about which he or she cares nothing, and I have to say, "Why do you ask that when you couldn't care less?" Or perhaps I am answering a question and the master of ceremonies, e.g., Eric Goldman on a program ludicrously called "The Open Mind," suddenly becomes fearful because I am criticizing the network or even introducing a sexual subject; he tries to cut me off. Then there is nothing for it but to take him by the arm and say, "Look, I'm not being paid for this. I'm here because your station has pre-empted the audience and I have something to say. I *will* say it." This is unpleasant. But the worst is when I am completely snowed and emasculated by the format—it is too quick and glib for me—and then I determine not to go back there. (When there has been a battle, they won't have me back there!)

It is also dangerous to make a recording, for they will

likely cut out your meaningful sentences. They pledge not to, but I have known them to lie. The last time I was approached by a man from CBS, I said I would require a forfeit. This of course was unheard of and impossible. Does anyone have a suggestion how we can use their media and yet protect ourselves from being edited and abused?

Let me mention a sobering incident of another kind. Last winter some of us engaged in a series of peace demonstrations in New York. At one, I was picketing my publisher with a sign, "Take Time Off to Stop the Cold War," and a friend, Jules Rabin, who had walked from San Francisco to Moscow, came by to march up and down with me in the snow. Then Ben Grauer of NBC-TV came to cover the picketing and he started, predictably, by asking me, "Why don't you picket the Kremlin?" "That's odd you ask me that," I said, "since my friend Jules here just did. Why don't you ask him that question?" With a sour face, Grauer had the camera turned on him, asked a brusque question, and received an interesting reply. *Yet this dramatic incident was edited out for the broadcast.* I cannot but think that this was dishonest reporting. It must occur often. It is a peculiarly deadly kind of censorship, since people take photographs as signs of reality. Editing like this keeps reinforcing a stereotype and finally, alas, makes it be all the reality there is.

When Robert Wool, the editor of *Show,* asked me to write something for him, I at first refused, for I had nothing to say.* Then I recalled my experience at Knox, and

---

* The kind of criticism of popular culture that even a good journalist like Dwight Macdonald does, seems to me to be futile. To expose our society, one does not need to look at movies, etc.; it is more direct to look out the window or at the front page of the *Times.* And if the aim is to make the mass-audience more critical of what it swallows, the worst possible method is for a respected man to take the products seriously—or ironically—and then cavil about them. Perhaps, however, Macdonald *does* take them seri-

I suggested that it might be interesting and useful to report on a couple of hours of the TV as I actually experienced them with an innocent eye, at least a TV-innocent
eye. The editor agreed to this with mild enthusiasm. In
order to get the right tone, I decided to watch the common
or household variety, rather than the big evening programs
or the dramas. (Upon the advice of John Oatfield of *Radio-
TV Reports* I chose March 28th from 11 A.M. to 2 P.M.;
and I went to my brother's where there is a television machine.)

Again to my surprise, my response was nothing like
disgust or anger; it was rather a mixture of sadness and
compassion for the anxiety, the tension, and the fright
manifested on the screen, in most of the persons, in almost
all of the format and timing, and in the texture of the
commercials. (I shall mention exceptions.) In one case, as
I shall explain, I was myself swept into the anxiety and it
took, I guess, a year off my life. Let me describe four programs.

The first was not, on the whole, anxious-making. It was
a Giving Away of Commodities to the one on a panel of
contestants who guessed closest to their list price. This was
stupid but not unpleasant. The contestants were eager for
the commodities, or at least interested in them, as well as
in doing well, so the contest was not merely a painful
competition. The lady who won, and had won the day before, had a shrewd eye and a greedy joy that were quite
appropriate to the game and marked her as a champion in
this kind. A gentleman—he was in insurance—seemed to

---

ously, in which case there is nothing further to say; it is his privilege. I
was once a movie-reviewer myself, on *Partisan Review*, twenty years ago.
My first month, there was, blessedly, Chaplin's *Great Dictator*, worth writing about. The next month I looked in vain, and finally covered a festival
of D. W. Griffith at the Museum of Modern Art and reviewed a book on
it by Iris Barry. But the third month I was altogether at a loss; I wrote a
theoretical article on the esthetics of the Shape of the Screen; and gave up.

hedge his guesses according to the probabilities of the game rather than interest in the commodites; he did less well. A third, a Jewish lady from Brooklyn, did poorly because the commodities were not really for her: they were spring-time suburban items, patio furniture, a golf-cart, a line of Robert Hall dresses; if they had been Ohrbach's, she would have priced them on the nose. The master of ceremonies of all this acted the zany, putting on a funny hat, etc., and this was what it was. Indeed, the only elements out of context were the commercials, and they were bad. The zany suddenly assumed a solemn tone and said, "*Remember* that in Krispy crackers the flavor and crispness are twice protected," and he gave a box a little proprietary tap. A Heinz commercial was frantic in its cutting and gave one indigestion, too quickly showing stalks of rice in a field—in a hand—a baby—a glass container—a box; one could not take a breath. This ad and another used the buddy-buddy "You see" that I find insulting: "You see the folks at Heinz have been blending. . . . You see Milk of Magnesia does more for you." During the course of this show also, we were assured, by an actor dressed in a white jacket, that "90 percent of doctors themselves take aspirin."

The next program, however, made me sad, compassionate, and ill. It was a sample of nursery-school, with a teacher and half a dozen four-year-olds. The essential idea was entirely false, for although most of the action was "for the children," everything was directed toward getting mama to buy at a certain "friendly" department store. E.g.: "So tell your mother to get this game at . . . the phone number is XY-z 8222"—this to tiny children! But the agony of the show was the suffering of the teacher. She seemed competent to handle the children, but not in this format, in front of a camera, where every second had to be chock-full. She did not stop rattling away. Every sentence was too fast. She was in a tightly controlled panic lest anything spontaneous occur, and she kept saying, "Now let's not go too far because we want to open the big door that goes into Wonderland"—"Let's not reach for our cookies *yet.*" Yet under these frantic circumstances, she still had to get them to perform and not freeze, and so she was continually tensely urging, "C'mon everybody, now we're going to have physical fitness fun. . . . C'mon all the Jacks fall down. . . . C'mon everybody, be children, everybody in Romper Room." (*Romper Room* was the name of this torture, though the little boys wore the usual long trousers and the girls proper frocks.) "C'mon everybody, let's sing *Chickadee happy and gay*—" and she would sing in a strained voice, but the children would be mum, or mumble, or make inhibited frightened gestures. Generally the children were wooden and brow-beaten; from time to time one would give a spasmodic skip or hop. Then a small lamb and goat were brought on, tugged by the leash to keep their noses in the camera. It was impossible, observing all this constraint and suffering, of animals, small children, and the hard-working woman, not to become quite ill. I was shocked at only one point, when the teacher left the group to demonstrate and speak for an ad, for a Green Thumb Plant Set. For some reason, also, the little nursery school kept reverting to nationalism and militarism, starting (age 4) with a flag salute and pledge of allegiance, and repeating, "C'mon now, be soldiers . . . walk like soldiers." I often wanted to switch this one off and spare myself, but soldier-like I stayed with it for this report.

Next was *Your First Impression,* again a game, consisting of guessing a Personality from a few clues. It was deft and not especially stupid, but unlike the Pricing Commodities game it had no relevance to the appetites of the contestants. They were there, apparently, simply to win. (I do not know if they were paid.) This made it a meaningless competition, to be merely skillful, merely to excel. What could the audience identify with in such a case, except an exercise in one-upping? In short, the contest was a gimmick, simply an expense of spirit, it had no animal or social reason for being. It was typically what Boorstin has called a "pseudo-event." Nevertheless, the half-hour had one satisfactory minute, the Ivory commercial. Unlike any other commercial I saw, this had a pleasant drawing and a nice plastic flow into the pictures of a baby and wash on the line, in subdued tone and texture, and with a reasonable pace of cutting. The network announcement, however, with its brass fanfare and zippy montage, had the usual ulcer-producing ugliness.

Finally, I watched a psychologist who answered letters from listeners, which were read rather obsequiously by a man probably on the staff of the station. Ordinarily, as an author in the field, I would expect to pay attention to such questions and answers; but this particular doctor made it difficult, because she allowed herself to project nothing from the screen. She did not give her voice out to the listeners, nor did it come from deep enough in her throat to reveal herself. The studio had made her up to be a tidy image of suburban competence. Her smile, appearing after she had made a point, seemed primarily for herself and secondarily to say to me, "Bear with me; you see? we'll get through it." She behaved, to my judgment, as if a little beyond her depth, although she was of course perfectly adequate to the routine wisdom allowable on such an occasion. It was the public role that was beyond her. (It would be beyond anyone.) But the astounding thing about Dr. Brothers was the movement of her body. She was entirely front, and when she moved, to turn to the reader of the letters, it was as a solid block. Sometimes the effect of this was ferocious. She did not move but moved herself. Her cheeks and brow were generally immobile while she moved her mouth; occasionally, however, at moments whose meaning I could not fathom, her brow would suddenly furrow with intense questioning perplexity that seemed to say, "Am I doing all right?" Her shoulders were held firm, so her hand gestures, again, did not flow or spring from her but were pushed forward. She had one commercial pitch—for Office Temporaries, "Use your spare time profitably"—and this was disastrously deflating of her precarious authority; she should resolutely refuse to say it. Professionals do not plug ads. On the whole, the effect of the performance (on me) was the unease that arises in the presence of irrelevant and misplaced effort; I felt a compassionate desire to cut the song-and-dance and get to the reality, the person herself who was over-controlling all this behavior; to ask her, "What is the matter, dear?"

By and large the tension and anxiety in these presentations seem to start from the commercials and spread over all the rest. I suppose the effect is inevitable in the commercials themselves, for their time is evidently scheduled to the second and greed crams them over-full. But the persons also are caught in the wooden framework and generally express the strain of it. If this painful feeling is not experienced by the spectators (I do not know if it is), it is because they are glued in it themselves. I could not habitually watch these programs without emotional damage.

I doubt that the whole can be remedied. Any attempt to "correct" the conditions I have been describing must result in some other phony format, some other wooden framework. On the other hand, to achieve documentary naturalism, or the feeling and imagination of art, would require allowing the spontaneous, the unscheduled, the empty, or the honest.

[*In the next issue of* Dissent, *Frank B. Gibney informed the Editors that it was not Huntington Hartford, the President of* Show, *but himself, the Publisher, who had rejected my essay, "because it was not very good." In my opinion, publishers and presidents ought to let editors do the editing, and stick to their own business of writing checks.*]

2

WAR

•

November 16, 1961

Mr. John F. Kennedy
The White House
Washington, D.C.

Dear Mr. President,

I must object to a government statement, in the bulletin on Radio-active Fallout distributed by the Office of Civil and Defense Mobilization. Speaking of fallout, the bulletin says, "It is merely a physical fact of this nuclear age. It can be faced like any other fact."

This sentence is false and misleading. Fallout—in the context in which this pamphlet is issued—is a *social* fact, not a physical fact. The advertising-man's tone, combining cajolery and inevitability, is quite contemptible on this subject.

May I ask you to have the passage deleted in subsequent printings.

Sincerely,

[*This was answered from Battle Creek, by the Office of Civil Defense, and I wrote again as follows:*]

•

December 1, 1961

Mr. John F. Kennedy
The White House

Dear Mr. President,

On Nov. 16 I wrote to you objecting to a sentence in a Civil Defense bulletin saying, "Fallout is merely a physical fact of this nuclear age. It can be faced like any other fact." I pointed out that this sentence was false and misleading, since fallout, in this context, is a *social* fact. I was offended also by the advertising-man's tone, combining cajolery and inevitability, which on this subject is contemptible. I asked you, finally, to have the passage altered in subsequent printings.

Today I receive from a Mr. G. D. Rich of the Office of Civil Defense in Battle Creek an extraordinary letter pointing out that "Many physical facts have social implications. It is important that all of us recognize the social implications of physical facts, whether they result from natural causes or the acts of man. . . . Please be assured that we are concerned with the social implications of the physical effects of fallout."

Perhaps I did not make my objection clear (I think I did). I am not interestingly concerned with the social effects *after* the bombs have fallen, but with the social nature of dropping the bombs. "Physical facts that result from the acts of men," as Mr. Rich puts it, are social facts in their essence.

Therefore I must reiterate my request that you delete or alter the passage. Mr. Rich tells me in his letter that a reprinting of the pamphlet is "unlikely." If so, I wish you would find other means to disabuse the public of this officially sponsored falsehood.

Sincerely,

cc: Mr. G. D. Rich

•

October 6, 1961

Mr. Morris Iushewitz
Board of Education
New York, N.Y.

Dear Mr. Iushewitz,

Will you please look into the following situation? At the Bronx High School of Science there were, in the first eighteen days of school, *four* shelter drills. The form of one such drill was kneeling and holding a book over one's head, an interesting medievalism for a school of science! Several of the youngsters—my son Mathew among them—declined to cooperate in these drills and quietly stood apart. Yesterday the principal, Mr. Taffel, threatened them with "police action," and today four of them, including Mathew, were suspended from classes.

Surely such a penalty is excessive and uneducational. The use of these shelters—even if they existed—is debatable; the drills are humiliating; it is very likely unwise to get people used to the idea of nuclear war; it is certainly unwise to break the morale of dissent. When an issue is as dubious as this, it is stultifying to all the youngsters of the school to exact such heavy penalties.

School authorities must have power to discipline, but the aim must always be to educate, and everything depends on the kind and degree of discipline. What is the advantage of excluding these students who are earnest in their work, independent in their thought, and motivated by the highest ideals of youth? It is a disastrous social policy to alienate them from the common life; and it is a stupid—and dangerous—educational policy to frighten the others into conforming.

I have received a note from Mr. Giles M. Rae, in charge of discipline at the school, about my son. This warns me that "behavior of this type can do immeasurable harm to his future possibilities for recommendations and college entrance." It is all down on the Permanent Record. In my opinion this is pretty outrageous pressuring, especially considering the insecure and ambitious temperament of many of the parents at Bronx Science. This attitude of the Organized System is not, however, calculated to make creative scientists.

I have spoken with Mr. Taffel, the principal. The chief burden of what he said seems to be his fear of the situation getting "out of control." I am sure my boy has no wish to disobey the school's authority, so I have urged him to obey all orders except the substantive one of the shelter-drill itself; I cannot ask him to move his feet in a way which he thinks to be senseless and evil.

Dissent and high principle must be tested by hardship, and obviously my boy is prepared for hardship. But it is the duty of educators to see to it that this necessary process is reasonable, that it does not alienate, break the spirit, or create a general atmosphere of fear.

Sincerely,

cc: Clarence Senior

[*The youngsters were reinstated on the next school day and given permission not to take part in future drills. They were promised that no record would be kept. As of October 1962, however, the official policy at some schools, e.g. Charles Evans Hughes High School, is to make a notation on the Permanent Record.*

What is most significant, however, is that despite their "victory," the pacifiists at Bronx Science could not greatly increase their adherents, not beyond 12, even though there was to be no penalty. The students at Science, and their parents, vaguely or clearly understand that their "future" is bound up with war industries and the National Defense Education Act.]

•

[Strangely, it was not till a year later that a case came up involving the conscientious objection of a teacher. When it was called to my attention I wrote to the Board again, as follows. I also got in touch with the Assistant Superintendent in charge of Junior High School 44, and there was an amusing exchange. He pointed out to me that if 95% of the teachers acted like Mr. Council, it would be impossible for the Principal to cover the classes! He apparently did not look forward with joy to the fact that we would then be rid of nuclear war! It is very difficult for administrators to look beyond the difficulties of administration. It is quite impossible for them to imagine that the objectors are serious.

I must report that in both the Bronx Science case and the Council case, the New York Post *ran forthright and useful libertarian editorials.]*

November 5, 1962

Clarence Senior
Board of Education, New York City

Dear Clarence,

Will you please inform me of the official policy in the Civil Defense business. As you know, a number of cases have come up.

A parent at J.H.S. 44, Mrs. Janet Karlson, called me

today about James Council; I told her to put the matter on our local agenda. (Probably November 19.) Council sent me a copy of the Principal's letter to Mrs. O'Brien (in charge of Personnel at headquarters), in which she says that if Council reports to any other school, "she would inform the Principal immediately." I do not know if Council fulfilled all punctilio about having the children covered; he did, however, notify the Principal before the drill. Frankly, in my opinion he is educationally completely in the right. It is out of the question for a teacher not to have the right, and encouragement, to proceed according to his conscience in such an important matter. Otherwise the children will never know what real citizenship is. They must be able to see dissent in action.

Likewise, I have today had several calls concerning the incident at Francis Lewis High School, where, it seems, the Principal suspended seven children—"indefinitely, until they promise never to do it again"—for nothing but wearing some arm-bands. I am told that he had previously threatened them, and had recently suspended another for wearing an arm-band. He had written on the Permanent Record "psychologically insubordinate" (!) instead of the honest factual statement, "suspended for wearing a pacifist arm-band." Such handling seems to me altogether inadmissible and out of proportion. According to my (student) informant, the Principal ranted and pounded and declared that we must at once bomb Moscow.

Now at Bronx Science, as you know, the policy is that the students need not participate in the drills at all, but may go to the Principal's office. Their names are taken, with what consequence I do not know. Likewise, on a visit to Charles Evans Hughes High, I was informed by the Principal that the students do not have to participate— though they are not aware of this, and he sees no reason to make them aware of it.

Obviously there is confusion and inconsistency. Please tell me what, if any, the Board's policy is: (a) on student non-participation in a drill, (b) on teacher non-participation, with adequate notice.

Further, whatever the policy, would it not be above-board to have the Principal inform the students as to what the policy is?

Best wishes,

cc: to Lloyd Garrison, Board of Education

[*This rash of new cases seems partly to have been the result of the Cuban crisis of October 1962. Many people, parents and children, have come to the feeling that we can't go on this way; the entire situation is too dangerous. At Bronx Science High School, the number of non-participants during two drills at this period rose to 27 and 35.*]

•

[*Local School Board 6 and 8 advised the Board of Education to re-instate Council and to reconsider the entire matter of the Civil Defense Drills which a majority of our local board considered to be uneducational. This was a thorny request, since the State law required such drills. The Board of Education circumvented us by giving the matter back to the Acting Superintendent of Schools, Dr. Bernard Donovan.*]

December 21, 1962

Max Rubin
Chairman of the Board of Education
New York, New York

Dear Mr. Rubin:
The press release of Dr. B. Donovan on rejecting James Council's appeal contains a proposition so ill-considered as to be almost slanderous. Please get some kind of retrac-

tion. But I am even more alarmed about the kind of mentality revealed, which I had also heard from Dr. Becker, the assistant principal of Junior High School 44.

After giving his grounds for upholding Council's dismissal, Dr. Donovan commences the following *obiter dictum*:

> "It does not appear that the supervision of children during a shelter drill in any way violates a conscientious objection to nuclear warfare. As a matter of fact, Mr. Council's statement that he would participate in shelter drills if there were an actual emergency but not during the practice drills, casts considerable doubt upon the philosophical soundness of his conscientious objection to shelter drills as an adjunct of nuclear warfare. His willingness to participate in time of war would seem to make his refusal to prepare for such participation wilful disobedience rather than conscientious objection."

This reasoning is fantastic. If Council were *not* prepared to do what he could for the children in an actual nuclear bombing, he would be morally insane. How can Donovan conceive of anybody's maintaining "conscientious objection" at a point where the demands of charity override all personal morals altogether? And indeed, Council's two choices here are philosophically logical and Donovan doesn't know what he's talking about. I assume that Council's rejection of the phony drills, like my own, is because they are a (psychological) preparation for nuclear war by making such a horror thinkable. If despite our efforts to stop it, the terrible eventuality occurred, one obviously could no longer be warding it off, and a moral man would prefer to die responsibly with his charges, like any captain.

In my opinion, it is intolerable that on a matter of this difficulty the Board of Education should allow an administrative mentality to judge and decide. From such mentality we can expect nothing but the rigid application of rule quite beyond moral or scientific reality. Let me inform you of an exchange with Dr. Becker, testifying before Local Schools Boards 6 and 8:

QUESTION: Council *said* he would not take part in the drill. He dismissed his class and left the room before the homeroom class arrived for the drill. Why hadn't the principal sent a covering teacher?

DR. BECKER: She thought that he would not go through with it. (!)

There you have it. It is apparently inconceivable to such bureaucratic administrators that there is any reality beyond their ruling and chain of command. This constitutes an army or a factory; it is not a school.

Allow me therefore to ask you

1. to get a retraction of Dr. Donovan's offending paragraph,

2. to censure the Principal of Junior High School 44 for her cavalier handling of the situation.

3. to deal with the Council case before the Board itself, as a matter of *policy,* as it deserves because of its subtlety and importance. In such cases we need community *mind,* not top-down decision.

Sincerely,

cc: Clarence Senior
    Lloyd Garrison
    Gerald Coleman, Chairman of Board 6 and 8

[*The structural issue here is very interesting. Usually when there are lay boards controlling a professional staff, one has to defend the professionals against the meddling of prejudiced and ill-informed laymen. But in a system the size of*

*New York's, the "professional" staff is not professional at all,
but is an administrative bureaucracy; and it happens that the
present "lay" Board of Education in New York is, by and large,
more philosophical and truly professional.*

*[The Board did in fact then consider the case and upheld
the teacher's dismissal, Clarence Senior dissenting.]*

●

October 1, 1961

Editor, *The New York Post*

Dear Sir,

Since many people seem eager to spend money for fallout shelters, may I suggest that these be used to alleviate
the housing shortage. Owners could rent out their shelter
to poor families—in many cases this is better housing than
they now have. The rent would reimburse the cost of the
shelter and there might even be a profit. The lease could
provide for immediate evacuation in case of a bombing.

Yours,

[This was printed on October 5th.]

●

May 20, 1960

Editor, *Columbia University Forum*

Dear Sir,

Allow me to object to Stephen P. Dunn's calling the
attempt of the *Golden Rule* to sail into the Pacific bomb-
waters, "a dramatic and colorful 'stunt.' " Precisely in the
context of excessive organization that he is talking about,
where we lose touch with every real job, task, or goal, in
a fog of organized procedures, and where the most important and obvious goods are therefore astoundingly lost by

default, it is certainly relevant (and not merely dramatic) to engage in non-violent direct action.

But actions like the *Golden Rule* or the recent beautiful resistance to the spurious Civil Defense are, indeed, even simpler. They are what used to be called Bearing Witness. There are situations, different for different persons, in which it is impossible to live and breathe, to continue to be oneself, unless one affirms and acts out the contrary, at whatever risk and however "foolishly." If such action is a stunt, it is in the sense that Kierkegaard calls the man of faith an acrobat.

Mr. Dunn is concerned for the sociological image of the Committee for a Sane Nuclear Policy, that its members not be regarded as cranks. There is a place in public education for "the highly respectable tradition of democratic agitation: letters and advertisements in the press, communications to public figures, etc." that he speaks of. But I think he is making the mistake of believing that the world abstracted for sociology is the world itself. The world consists of men before it consists of committees. When ordinary common sense—e.g. "it's pretty stupid to poison the atmosphere"—is called crankiness, psychological wisdom is *not* to try to change an image, but to shake somebody hard by the shoulders and say, Snap out of it.

Yours,

[This was printed in the Summer issue, 1960.]

•

[I am a "sponsor" of a pacifist movement called the World-wide General Strike for Peace, which springs from the thought that the Cold War is integrally involved with most of the economy and culture of our society, and that we by our co-operation give energy to the drift toward destruction. The General Strike is a call for non-cooperation.

Some of the following letters are concerned with this movement.]

November 10, 1961

Editor, *The Village Voice*
New York

Dear Sir,
I am in general agreement with Emile Capouya's letter of November 9 supporting the strike against nuclear war on January 29. I think, however, that his suggestion of a march down Fifth Avenue somewhat misses the point. Each person ought to picket his own place of work, where he is on strike. We want to convey the idea that we can't go on with Business As Usual, in circumstances that threaten any business whatever. My hope is that, on reflection, many would refuse to cross such picket lines. I myself shall picket Random House or Macmillan.
Following this same reasoning, about 70 instructors and professors at Cornell are going to devote their class time on Nov. 17 to discussing nuclear war. I would urge teachers in New York City to set a day and do likewise.

Yours,

[*Printed Nov. 16, 1961. During the strike, we combined both Mr. Capouya's suggestion and mine. Bennett Cerf at Random House sent me out a cup of coffee, since it was snowing. I think Tolstoy would have enjoyed this.*]

•

February 2, 1962

United Nations

Dear Secretary U Thant,
May I make a complaint about the handling of demonstrations at the United Nations?

In our General Strike for Peace—sponsored by Bertrand Russell, Herbert Read, Pitirim Sorokin, Dorothy Day, and others—we obtained a police permit to picket peaceably in the U.N. plaza on January 31st. The purport of our signs was that both the United States and the Union of Soviet Socialist Republics were pursuing a disastrous course, and we urged the peoples of the world to try to get them to relax the Cold War. When we arrived, the New York police shunted us to the little island across First Avenue at 42nd—and barricaded off half the space at that!

The U.N. is chartered in the name of the people of the world. I do not understand why we cannot express our views and wishes at its doors, in the ordinary public area. If I may speak also as a critic of architecture (and a friend of Le Corbusier), that vast empty plaza becomes a frigid architectural monstrosity if it is never animated by the assemblage of people, whether for jubilation, indignation, or petition. I am sure the architect would be distressed.

Will you please explain your policy on this matter?

Sincerely,

[*The Secretary answered that this matter belonged to the New York Police Department.*]

•

[*The New York Times refused $5,600 and to print our broaside for the General Strike. About 20 of us picketed their 43rd Street office in protest. Their report of the picketing was unsatisfactory.*]

February 3, 1962

Editor, *The New York Times*

Dear Sir,

I must complain about your account of the picketing of the *Times* on January 26, protesting your refusal of an

ad for the General Strike for Peace. Your news account
again repeated your explanation that you could not print
a call to "action" that "might" create a disturbance. But,
as you knew, the police had given permits for every activity scheduled in the ad. It is not up to the *Times* to decide
what "might" create a disturbance. Your objection to a
call to "action" is altogether inconsistent. You will gladly
print ads that say "buy" and "work", but you are unwilling to print calls that say "do not buy or work for an hour,
a day, a week" in order to show that we will not indefinitely cooperate with a society committed to the Cold War.
Legally, you can run your business as you wish, but then
you should not pose as a great newspaper.

Yours,

cc: Judge Frederick van Pelt Bryan

[*This was neither printed nor answered. I am at a loss as to
how these gentlemen live with themselves.*]

•

August 30, 1962

Editor, *The New Leader*

Dear Sir,

I am bemused by Michael Harrington's sentence, in his
article on the New Peace Movements, "Occasionally,
though—e.g. . . . the General Strike for Peace in New
York last January—the inspiration for these actions suffers
from an anarchist tinge." As a sponsor of GSP—and I
should be willing to be labeled as a community anarchist
—may I comment?

As a Socialist, Harrington must somewhere have heard
of the connection between War and the State. Certainly
the evidence of history must convince us that centralized

sovereignty and power have lived and grown by war readiness and war waging; and the more the Powers have aggrandized themselves, the more crashing the destruction. The present economy of the United States could not be described without the military-industrial complex as a crucial factor; American foreign relations are entirely in terms of bellicose power blocs and spheres of influence; to mention my own field, even our State-subsidized higher education is becoming increasingly apprentice-training for war-making.

Therefore, whether one knows it or not, any acts for peace, or even the remission of war, are in fact proposing a radical relaxing of centralized sovereignty and power as a way of organizing society. But this is anarchism. The advantage of being conscious about it is that one can then explore the functional regional arrangements, rather than power arrangements, that might make sense.

In November, the General Strike will ask people actively and explicitly to refuse to vote, except for the handful of candidates in the country who are unambiguously committed to immediate action towards peace.

Yours,

[*Printed in the following issue.*]

•

October 9, 1961

Editor, *Commentary*

Dear Sir,

Reading your symposium on "Western Values and Total War," I am astounded that, apart from one splendid paragraph of Mr. Morgenthau, there is no discussion of national sovereignty as the bottle-neck preventing a solution to the dilemma, and in fact creating and aggravating the dilemma. Yet the nation-state as we have it is simply what Lewis Mumford would call a baroque hangover. In this respect there is no difference between President Kennedy (and our power elite) and Louis the Fifteenth. Every time we speak of "we" and "they"—or of "unilateral" and "multilateral" disarmament—we essentially accept and affirm this disastrous conception. We are talking about States, not people.

The symposiasts are discussing absolute dangers—Prof. Hook seems to think that becoming "Red" is an absolute danger—and therefore it would be worthwhile to consider such merely relative "losses" as renouncing sovereignty in various combinations and degrees. (There are several other possibilities beside the supra-state that Mr. Morgenthau mentions.) Yet these possibilities have never been thoroughly explored in public discussion. Naturally such proposals are literally subversive; they involve lowering the flag. Is this why they are avoided by prestigious scholars?

On the other hand, the entire history of Western culture has to do with the motion among tribal, city, imperial, feudal, and national organization, and the dialectic of state-power and freedom. One is not giving up Western Values if one suggests that in present circumstances it would be wise to give up the United States of America.

Yours,

[*Printed in the issue of December 1961.*]

•

October 20, 1961

Editors, *Liberation*

Dear Sirs,

I am extremely disturbed by A. J. Muste's recounting of the pros and cons on Berlin: what the Russians think, what the Americans think, etc.; and the same holds for the frequent analyses of the subject by Erich Fromm. Given the desperate jeopardy we are in, what difference does it make *what* they think or what goes on at this level of thought? Any policies that involve such dangers are insane and are not policies at all. By human beings they should be dismissed as utterly irrelevant. We want no part of it, period. How the devil can one "explain" setting off new bombs when such explosions are a universal misfortune? To involve the reader in the intricacies of such "explanations" simply muddies the water. Contrast the clear and relevant rhetoric and reason of Bertrand Russell in the same October issue.

Because of his long and honorable career in the polemics and analyses of the politics of our century, A. J. has a propensity (I hope not fatal) to continue in the same strain, although we are no longer discussing a "political" question.

When he uses such terms as "unilateral" or "multilateral" action, he obscures our course of action. In the issue of nuclear war, there is no "we" and no "they," there are only human beings. If, as seems likely, the warring is implicit in the existence of national sovereignties like Russia, France, Nigera, the United States, etc., let us try to lower these flags at once.

I have had the same misgivings about the discussions in the *News-Letter* of the Committees of Correspondence and have so complained; but they do not publish my complaint. They do not seem to realize that there is a time *not* to rehash what is on the front page of *The New York Times*.

Yours,

[*Printed in the issue of Nov. 1961.*]

•

[*This is a leaflet written for the Second Call for a General Strike for Peace and distributed near the polls on Election Day, 1962.*]

The governments of the world have put us in the danger of nuclear total catastrophe and are wasting wealth and destroying health and spirit in waging the Cold War. Especially, of course, the United States and Soviet governments; but it is likely that the Common Market government will soon be an equally fearful third.

The Soviet government proceeds with no democratic check by its people. But in waging war and making deadly war-preparations, the United States government proceeds almost equally unchecked. For almost 100% of the candidates of the overwhelmingly major parties, however much they slightly differ in other respects, are unanimous in this crucial respect. The electorate has no choice to vote for peace. Like the Soviet government, our government drifts toward catastrophe as one bloc. (It is only in England, among the sovereign nations of the nuclear club, that there is any party strength toward peace, and *this has come about because of the massive civil disobedience of English pacifists.*)

Therefore, to vote for *any* candidates in this present election—except for a tiny few who have proved their will to peace by their records and their campaigns—is to legitimize with the popular will the insane policies of the nuclear nations. Since the government as such means war, *do not vote at all,* especially for national candidates. (In New York City there are one acceptable and five somewhat acceptable candidates, listed below.)

The vote is the most essential act of political societies. It is the act by which, in small or large communities, the citizens create the kind of world they want to live in, so far as this can be done by political means. Then it is a sacrilegious farce when the vote has come to mean rubber stamping one of two rival candidates who both share a policy that no citizen can sanely will. On the other hand, we cannot *merely* abstain from voting, for voting is too important, too existential an act. We therefore urge the citizens to engage in *active non-voting.* Picket the polls with your protests. Urge others not to vote and explain why.

A vote invests the Cold War and the nuclear war with legitimacy. Refuse it.

Support the General Strike for Peace. Boycott civilian goods produced by big war producers. Don't vote except for Peace candidates.

The following candidate has answered a General Strike questionnaire indicating that he is opposed to all Cold War policies: Oscar Gonzalez-Suarez, Congress, Republican, 22nd Congressional District.

In addition, the following candidates are committed to opposing the Cold War on some important issues though not fully committed to a peace and disarmament platform:

Martin B. Dworkis, Congress, Dem-Liberal, 17th Congressional District

John P. Hagan, Congress, Liberal, 23rd Congressional District

William F. Ryan, Congress, Democratic, 20th Congressional District

Manfred Ohrenstein, State Senate, Democratic, 25th State Senatorial District

James McNamara, Assembly, Liberal, 2nd A.D. Manhattan
(Results for New York City only)

•

[*Douglas Gorsline is one of the art editors of* Liberation, *a magazine of pacifist and somewhat anarchist tendency, of which I am an associate editor. The following is an answer*

58 :

to a letter of his chastising others of us for not taking part in the Peace Conference in Moscow, 1962]

June 19, 1962

Editor, *Liberation*

Dear Sir,

I am immensely in agreement with Doug Gorsline's passionate plea for Americans opposed to nuclear war to ally themselves with other peoples; and in general for Americans to re-join humanity and realize that other peoples have different views and, in many ways, better ways of life. Also, there is certainly a kind of comedy in the way our unilateral writers and organizations prove their purity from communism by attaching an anti-Russian rider to every blast at the Cold Warriors of the United States; or the Byzantine symmetry with which we picket the American and Russian embassies.

I doubt, however, that "International" efforts and congresses provide an answer, so long as we do not distinguish between the peoples of the world and the sovereign states. The Moscow conference is, practically speaking, under the auspices of a sovereign probably as much committed to the Cold War as our own, though differently—the U.S.A. operates more in the line of containment and profiteering, the U.S.S.R. of fishing in muddy waters and expanding. It seems clear that we shall not have peace until we get rid of the entire system of those powers, in Washington, Moscow, Paris, Bonn, etc.; and indeed, until we cease to think in terms of "power" altogether, including profits and expanding economies, and return to the ideas of human function, regional planning, and brotherhood.

To put it paradoxically, the only pacifist groups that could reasonably operate in the atmosphere of a state-approved Congress would be those like SANE, which believe they can talk practically to President Kennedy and so might as well talk to Premier Khrushchev; or, again, members of the Council of Correspondence, like Dr. Fromm, who still have hopes in an accommodation of the Great Powers. In my opinion, there will be no such accommodation unless the pressures of the peoples of the world begin to make the sovereigns shaky; and if the peoples can exert that much pressure, they can diminish "power" altogether.

Suppose a genuine radical pacifist (like Doug Gorsline) were at the Moscow Congress. Would he not exclaim about the horrible increase in the number of capital crimes in the Soviet Union, just as he cries out about the racism here? (I think these are fair equivalents.) The way of life of peace cannot be dissociated from these other matters. And if we consider the matter in this light, it is not fair to say that the "great majority" of at least the unilateralists are clinging to jobs, etc., if they devote their efforts mainly to the home-front. Our responsibility is obviously greatest with what is closest, and where we know from bitter experience the organic connections among the war-policy, the economy, the mass-media, the urbanism, the law, etc. The different peoples of the world must necessarily mind their own business of this kind for themselves and mostly by themselves. Needless to say, it is only by solidarity in a world community in fact trying to live better that any people can have strength and hope. But how hard it is to express and cement this solidarity! The march to Moscow was a remarkable achievement. More typical, I fear, is the kind of effort of the General Strike for Peace, that sends off bales of its leaflets translated into every tongue, but Lord knows what happens to most of those leaflets.

I doubt that "virtuous pacifism" is so officially acceptable as Doug thinks. My prediction is that the legal penalties are going to get stiffer, the firings from jobs more frequent, the news blackout more total. As Arthur Krock put it in *The New York Times*, "The intellectuals and pacifists . . . out of sincere conviction . . . will provide one of the explanations for the decline of the West." In my opinion, the profound reason why pacifists are called "communists" is just inwardly to deny that they are sincere and rational, that is pacifists. And we shall see the day when the "misguided idealists" are going to be more obnoxious than the communists, who at least have the decency to join in the Cold War.

But let me end with my agreement of the beginning. It is indispensable that the Americans learn how they look to others, especially to peoples who are not mesmerized by war-games. *Liberation* could perform a great service by printing regular reports of us from abroad. Our own self-criticism is acute, but necessarily we have blinders. We have a lot to learn.

Yours,

[*Printed in Summer 1962.*]

•

March 8, 1959

Editor, *The New York Times*

Dear Sir,

I was saddened to read in the *Times* of March 6 that the wavelength of our satellite Discoverer IV "has been withheld for unexplained reasons of military 'security.'"

When these moons first were launched, although we were chagrined that the Russians beat us to it, nevertheless our overwhelming sentiment was enthusiastic wonder and pride at these achievements of mankind. We were enthusiastic when our men got back into the great race. What a pity if now we, and our children, should be robbed of our grand and ingenuous excitement by debasing these feats to the level of the cold war and business as usual.

Millions of the public money are spent on these experiments; and no one is so mean-spirited as to begrudge the expense for so grand an adventure as going to the moon and the planets. But it is a very different public tone when the money is voted because of fear.

For God's sake, let us not lightly destroy the few humane feelings we have that make life in our society worth living.

Yours,

[*The* Times *found no space for this.*]

●

January 14, 1962

Editor, *Sunday Book Review,*
The New York Times

Dear Sir,

Sidney Hook asserts that Bertrand Russell "charges, without proof, that the airman who gave the signal for the release of the Hiroshima bomb was railroaded to an insane asylum by American authorities because he regretted his action." Professor Hook's insinuation that there is no "proof" is entirely uncalled for. From the time that the Austrian philosopher Guenther Anders became interested in the astounding modern tragedy of Major Eatherly, the facts have had wide publicity; it was from Anders that Russell learned of the incidents; Robert Jungk researched the story again and his account, printed a year ago in Brussels, has been importantly noticed in the Canadian and American press. (There is a concise recapitulation in *Liberation,* January 1962.)

When Hook insultingly ridicules Lord Russell's complaint that Truman has been "unrepentant," he has renounced philosophy and humanism. What is the case? Whether or not Hiroshima and Nagasaki can be strategically justified, the fact remains that our government produced those bombs and that now we, like the rest of the world, exist in a state of chronic emergency and anxiety. Should not this pattern of retribution be a subject of thoughtfulness and mourning? Has the world heard one word of such mourning from Mr. Truman, Mr. Eisenhower, or Mr. Kennedy? It is the part of a philosopher and scholar to regard our destiny *sub specie eternitatis* and *sub specie humanitatis* and not merely, like Professor Hook, according to the exigencies of the Cold War.

Yours,

[*This was printed in sadly abridged form.*]

•

Date?

Editor, *The New York Post*

Dear Sir,

The Post is to be congratulated for Joseph Barry's coverage of the Jeanson trial in Paris, but I think that Barry does not analyze the situation precisely. There are two different issues: 1. Dissenting from the Algerian War by every means, including civil disobedience, draft-refusal, etc. 2. Giving active aid to the Algerian rebels. If I were a Frenchman I hope I should engage in the first of these, for the war *cannot* solve the problem. It is an endless drain of youth and wealth; it has led to horrors and insane cruelty. Finally it is necssary to say, "Enough! I won't."

Yet there *is* a real problem in Algeria. Three million French are at stake and no doubt the lives of many thousands of them. Perhaps the problem is insoluble, but one must hope and exhaust every possibility, for instance the enormous financial sacrifice of emigration. This is morally very different from directly aiding one's country's enemy to force a peace. To give an analogy: Burke and Fox spoke up for the Americans in parliament; Fox wore Washington's colors. But he would not, as an Englishman, have fought in Washington's army. The aim of protest must be to force one's government to renounce a ruinous course, it is not to defeat it in a war. Let the Algerians take care of themselves. The stand of the Jeanson circle confuses the moral issue, and this is characteristic of the violent activism that Sartre and his clique are prone to. Barry rightly admires French revolutionary patriotism, but he forgets the history of French treachery.

Sincerely,

[*This was not printed.*]

•

[*I was associated with the Liberal Project, described in the following editorial that I wrote for* Liberation, *April 1962.*]

In 1959-60 about ten fairly rational Democratic congressmen modestly decided that they didn't have any new ideas, and they asked a number of professors and writers who might have some, including myself, to contribute them as possible bases for bills. This was the Liberal Project. We dare not name the congressmen lest we do them —those who survived 1960 or have other jobs in Washington—irreparable damage by mentioning them with approval in *Liberation*. They are in enough trouble already, for now the foreign-policy volume has been published, with characteristic proposals by Charles Osgood, Stuart Hughes, Frank Tannenbaum, etc., and a wild cry has gone up in the Senate and the House to destroy the sponsors of these "most dangerous recommendations I have ever seen—they go beyond the Communist line" (William Miller, National Chairman of the Republican party). Besides, it seems, there are twenty-two "secret" Liberal Project members who must be smoked out. The dangerous recommendations, needless to say, are simply efforts to relax the Cold War before many scores of millions are killed.

For our purposes, what is interesting in this party tempest is to consider the fate of a little group like this in our governmental system. Often they have spoken out forthrightly enough in Congress—they include, e.g., the five who voted to abolish the House Un-American Activities Committee, and even a couple of pacifists. Mostly, however, their speeches go unreported in the press; most people do not know they exist. One of them explained to us, "If we were a bloc of 50, *The New York Times* would have to report our speeches. Ten or five aren't enough." Then another quoth somewhat as follows: "Our disaster was the election of Kennedy, for this completely fragmented the radical-liberal forces. In our districts we get elected by being pretty honest; the voters may disagree with us but they choose us; the electorate slowly improves; some of us ran ahead of the national ticket. If Nixon had won, a couple of dozen of us, perhaps even more, might have banded together openly as the core of a real opposition. But with the Democratic 'victory,' most of us are afraid to lose our chances of power or influence. What power? We wield no influence. In any way significant to the important issues, there was no difference between Nixon and Kennedy, but Kennedy's election was significant in destroying any real left." We would recommend this reasoning to the readers of the *New York Post*.

What is horrible about the present attack on the Liberal Project, however, is not the expected tone of William Miller or Everett Dirksen, but the craven behavior of the Liberals. According to *The New York Times* of March 26, "With the exception of Mr. Kastenmeier all the 'members' still in Congress now deny that there was ever any organization known as 'the Liberal Project.'" Representative O'Hara says, "I never met with this 'group' and discussed policy. Never never never never never." This Shakesperian vehemence is to disown essays written by Professors, Professors Emeriti, nay, Chairmen of Departments! It is then complained by the heavy thinkers in the Administration that there are no ideas, there are no alternatives to their ruinous course.

•

[*In the June 1962 issue of* Commentary, *I published an essay called "The Ineffectuality of Some Intelligent People", trying to explain why certain very earnest religious groups and radical professors did not swing more weight and did not themselves act. This evoked a good deal of irritated correspondence. I give here my answers to three of the correspondents, printed in the October and November numbers.*]

Reply to Messrs. Maurer and Yager:

Messrs. Maurer and Yager fail to understand that we, both myself and my ineffectual professors, are convinced that the escalating Cold War is inherent in our present system: the sovereign states, the power politics, the use we make of technology, and our whole way of life. We need a far more revolutionary change than these gentlemen envisage. Also, by "we" and "they" we cannot mean NATO vs. the Soviet bloc, but the peoples of the world against the sovereigns and their corporate and state economies.

All this was taken for granted in my essay—I have developed it a hundred times elsewhere. My theme was that the professors are ineffectual because, though convinced of all this, they do not behave consistently with it and follow the hard consequences. These correspondents, however, want me to speculate and find "alternatives" (e.g. containment, a Berlin policy) within the very framework of wargames and power-politics that *itself* is deadly.

Mr. Maurer assumes, like most contemporary political scientists, that "power," power to coerce, license, authorize, etc., is of the essence of politics. A little social psychology would teach him, I think, that this kind of sovereign power is largely a reaction-formation to thwarted functioning and *thwarts functioning further*. (Normal politics deals with the constitutional relations of functional interests.) There is a problem of how to cope when large numbers of people and all of the leaders are subject to reactive power drives and the correlative projected fears; but certainly, to aggravate the psychology, e.g. by mutual defiance and deterrence, is a poor expedient. A good first step would be to withdraw support from the leaders. Mr. Yager, analogously, seems to think that the profit motivation is friendly to a functional use of machinery and a scientific way of life. If so, he is an astonishingly ignorant man. (I would recommend a survey of our own corporate economy and the study of authors like Veblen, Dewey, Kropotkin, Geddes, Mumford, etc.)

In 1938 (and in 1941-5), I was, with grief, a pacifist because I knew that after that war we should be faced with this war; so it has gone on, in the present style for a century; and the time to stop was then—and now. But I felt then, as I do now, that pacifism was meaningless unless it involved positive action in a different style of life altogether to drain energy from the madness and create a viable modern world. In a long series of books and articles I *have* proposed alternatives of *this* kind, "specific policies," with what social effect I do not know. (We have seen, however, the effects of being "realistic" in 1938 without trying to remedy the causes of 1938.) If, as Mr. Maurer says, "Hiroshima was the final blow in the war against Fascism," then that method of combatting fascism must have been the wrong method, since it led to such an instrument and has confronted us with today's retribution. (The actual berserk use of the bomb after the end of the European war was typical of the whole logistic mentality, blind to total meaning; and now we are drifting into a fascism of the majority anyway.) So I say the first stroke of unfinished business is to mourn. When Mr. Yager jokes about "tuning in tomorrow to learn the second stroke," it is really no joke: we mourn because we have lost and are baffled; in order to live on, we have to see in a different way, which we do not know. Also, when he asks am I "trying to tell the confused citizen that nuclear war can be prevented by his associating with disreputable causes?" my answer is, "In principle, yes."

I don't know what goes at the President's dinners; he has not invited me. But Mr. Yager's remarks about "sincere ties, gray flannels, and bridge tables," and about jails, are insulting to young friends of mine, are beneath contempt, and are unworthy of further notice.

Yours,

[*In* Commentary, *October 1962.*]

•

[*In criticizing this same article, Margaret Mead accused the editor of* Commentary *of terrible irresponsibility for passing a trivial error of fact of mine. I was referring to a recent conference of the American Association for the Advancement of Science.*]

Reply to Margaret Mead:

My actual conversation with Professor Mead was exactly as I reported it. I assumed, from her characteristically matriarchal tone, that she was at least their president. I thought wrong. The news about the 60,000 and the special Committee was conveyed to me at the time, and it was no doubt careless of me to imply to the readers of *Commentary* that the small articulate and "radical" group spoke for them all, even in its feeble proposition. I gave them the benefit of the doubt.

The rest of Professor Mead's present statement about the perplexities of the scientists is profoundly unimpressive. She knows as well as I that in the differing "scientific appraisals" there is a good deal of plain quackery and sleight-of-hand. For example, with regard to safe radiation-levels or the effect of the high-altitude explosions, the scientists do not know—and the logical behavior should be, therefore, for them concertedly to advise the decision-makers and the public that it is unwise to act. I have not heard this concert. Imagine if the pure food and drug laws and the building code were administered with equal lack of caution. In another kind of case, would Professor Mead deny that the seismic evidence on inspection has been made the football of diplomacy or mere propaganda? But most important—and this was the point of my essay —do those scientists who in fact appraise the data as very dangerous, then band together and threaten to strike? *Of course* I affirm that any special knowledge and function— teacher, physician, industrial worker, or mother of children —is prior to the law. *No* other social theory is tenable. Why would Professor Mead think otherwise?

I wonder if she realizes the colossal cynicism of her last sentence: "The bomb and its attendant technological innovations . . . give us an unprecedented opportunity for new types of research and new types of action." This means that these excellent brains are to be sidetracked into further ingenious investigations even though the enterprise as a whole is admittedly catastrophic.

[*In* Commentary, *November 1962.*]

3

REPRESSION

•

[*On a man convicted of murder.*]

August 1, 1962

Dear Governor Rockefeller,
Allow me to speak for clemency for Manfredo Correa.

Dr. Carl McGahee, the psychiatrist who examined Correa, is definite in his statement that Correa was maddened by a withdrawal crisis. Consider what is involved here. It is widely admitted that our narcotics laws and our handling of addiction are seriously imperfect. If we had, like the English, for instance, a predominantly medical approach to the problem, there would be less likelihood of the occurrence of cases like Correa's. As it is, however, our admittedly faulty institutions can drive a man to despair and madness; and we then exact a full vengeance for acts committed in despair and madness. But this makes our society operate precisely like an infernal machine, and I feel deeply uneasy about being a part.

You, sir, have the opportunity somewhat to humanize the situation in this case, and to allow time, nature, and benevolent attention a chance to help us all in our miserable circumstances. Please avail yourself of it.

Sincerely,

•

[*Pete Hamill, a feature writer for the* New York Post, *did a series on the Dangerous Parks of New York. The following was a personal letter to him.*]

October 13, 1961

Dear Pete,

May I point out some wrongheaded damage in your pieces on the parks? I'm pretty sure that it's unthinking on your part.

There is rather conclusive community-planning evidence that it's not the homosexuals (or, less importantly, winos) who drive others out of the parks; rather it works the other way: when an area is fairly deserted—whether a little used park, deserted docks at night, etc.—homosexuals go there hoping to meet their similars or others experimentally inclined or out for an easy, and perhaps pleasant, buck; chaps who for the most part seek out the spots with their eyes open. The mechanism is perfectly clear: the marginal, embarrassed and fearful group isolates itself, at the same time needing to be somewhere publicly available.

Now where else would you have them go? (I say "you" identifying you with some of your indignant interlocu-

tors.) Groups congregate in huge cities just in order to increase the chances of contact with the like-minded. There
must always be marginal spaces for the generally disap-
proved. What is the alternative to homosexuals haunting
empty parks? To jail or liquidate them all?

I am rather astounded, too, at the blithe way you report
the cops' plain clothes men. Will you spell out for yourself
the course of such entrapment as they practice?

Naturally in such a miserable set-up, there occurs plenty
of violence, blackmail, and bribery; and very little chance
of even a poor kind of satisfaction. It is in this respect that
your articles do social damage; for by your tone you accept and affirm the repressive atmosphere whose existence
increases the violence and blackmail, and that is the background for sexual troubles in the beginning. This is what
the Wolfenden Report was about. (An English parliamen-
tary report on amending the sex laws.)

I don't see any way you can amend damage done; but
use your head a little harder in the future.

Best wishes,

cc: Murray Kempton

[*Hamill thanked me for my letter and resolved to use his
head a little harder in the future.*]

•

[*I am struck, in this and some of the following pieces, by
my reference to the execution of Carryl Chessman. The long
years of cruel delay in that case brought into terrible clarity
the mechanical nature of capital punishment, analyzed so well
by Camus, for there could not even be remaining the emotional justification of vengeance. And for the same reason, one
could perceive with terrible clarity the settled and character-
ological nature of anti-sexual prejudice, for people had long*

years to think the matter over and get past their impulsive responses.]

May 7, 1962

Editor, *The New York Post*

Dear Sir,

Mrs. Franzblau's remarks (May 5) on the need to conceal the parents' nakedness are dangerously misleading. She refers to confusion, fright, and inferiority in the child's mind, but these do *not* spring from the experience of nakedness as such but from the confused, frightened, and frightening sexual attitude in the general culture that makes it impossible to integrate the child's sexual curiosity into the rest of his on-going education. The majority popular opinion in the Chessman case was a horrible example. A child has a better chance of threading the confusing maze of such a sadistic and pornographic culture if he has come from a bolder and franker home. I urge your psychologist to consider the happy results in the American Indian tribes reported by Dr. George Devereux, where from earliest infancy not only the parents' nakedness but their love-making are used as valuable studies for growing up. In general, Mrs. Franzblau would be a better psychologist if she were a better sociologist and more critical of our present mores.

Sincerely,

[*Not surprisingly, the* Post *found no room for these observations.*]

•

[*In the* Catholic Worker, *a religious pacifist paper, one of the editors, Robert Steed, expressed his dismay at the high proportion of letters urging capital punishment for Chessman. I wrote the following to explore the subject further.*]

May 1, 1960

Dear Robert Steed,

I don't think that your remarks on American puritanism (Catholic and Protestant) in the Chessman case, went far enough.

Though you and I would probably not see eye to eye on correct sexual morals, I think we would agree that the puritan inhibition goes beyond the order of nature. Now psychologically this transgression has specific consequences, of which vindictive sadism is the important one that appears in the tone of your hostile correspondents. The psychological mechanisms are partly as follows: The so-called "self-control" of the puritan is really a form of self-torture and rouses his natural resistance. Conquering this, the "self-controlling" tyrant feels himself great, victorious, grown-up, and self-righteous, even though the victim of his superiority is only his own cowering embodied soul. This particular conceit is, alas, very prevalent among our youth. In this unhappy internal clinch, it is of course the tyrant who controls the press: e.g. the harmless and inevitable dirtiness of sexuality—as Augustine said, "we are born among urine and feces"—is judged as disgusting; and universally felt urges, pornographically enlarged out of all proportion by the inhibition and repression that prevent a clear and sane experience of them, are judged as monstrous and damnable. Finally, when this uneasy internal stasis is disturbed by the thought of somebody *else* "getting away with something," the results are disastrous to charity, justice, and common sense: the self-righteous, "self-controlling" tyrant can now feel even grander in attacking this hellish enemy; all the stoked-up rage of frustration (for the hell is really within) can for a moment find relief by being vented as resentment against the scapegoat;

and pornographic images of sin and torture are not absent. This is vindictive sadism.

We both have faith, I am sure, that all this melancholy process can be cleansed away by charity, wisdom, compassion; but such gifts of the spirit seem to be rare in these issues. (Your figure of 75% of hostile letters is close to the national average in the Chessman case.) The advantage of careful analysis of how we behave and judge is to give us the saving sense that we may, after all, be wrong in our loudness. In the quiet we may hear better voices.

Sincerely,

[This letter was not printed, as explained in the following.]

•

[A communication to KULCHUR, #4, an advance-guard little magazine.]

May I comment on a couple of comments about me in your last issue?

Tuli Kupferberg quotes me as saying that "over 90% (95?)" of the readers of the *Catholic Worker* wanted to execute Chessman. My fading memory is that it was 70%. The young man who reported the figure in the *CW* was himself astonished and dismayed by it; so I wrote him a letter, for publication, explaining how Catholic sexual education in America must lead to this vindictiveness. My reasoning was somewhat as follows: A child defeated in his sexual expression identifies with his oppressor in order to fill up the psychic gap; he develops a conceit—strongly encouraged by his church—of having a "strong will" and "self control," as he torments himself and spaces out his masturbations on the calendar; and this conceited character triumphantly wreaks its vengeance against projected scapegoats. To my surprise this academic—and fairly irrefutable—explanation was not printed in the *CW*. The young journalist apologetically told me that, though he agreed with me, there was no use in even showing my letter to Dorothy Day because she would not consider printing anything about sex. To me, this makes the sanctimonious religiosity of the *CW* seem merely dirty proxy sex; and blasphemous, disowning the creation. It is time somebody said so.

Secondly, in an interesting discussion of pornography, Donald Phelps asks me a perceptive question about an essay of mine on the subject. He says that I "apparently feel" that my solution, "legalizing pornography," is "rather bold." My solution *is* bold, but not because of the acceptance of pornography, which is, as he points out, the social trend. My proposal is bold because of its proposition to *do nothing* in the face of an anxiety-producing situation; this goes counter to the obsessional American morality, that pours millions into the FBI. It is not "legalization" that can change attitudes; but the sense that in certain areas coercive law is quite irrelevant one way or the other would be an important change in attitude. My aim is to make the issue not a big deal. To my mind this is the crux of the sexual problem. Consider the vulgar misinterpretation of Freud. He did not mean to say that sex was an overwhelmingly determining factor; there were maybe six or seven great things, like safety, means of livelihood, knowledge, creator spirit, community, and including love and sex. But when sexuality is frustrated and repressed, then it distortedly colors and eroticizes everything else.

This brings me to the sage question of Donald Phelps. He asks how I would "attack the taste for bad pornography, which certainly is not solely the product of repressive censorship. Almost as deep-laid as the instinct for pornography is human laziness, seeking a cheap, simple, and easy substitute for something which, in any worthwhile form,

is demanding, complex, and hard." I have considerable respect for this kind of notion, though I ultimately disagree
with it. Morris Cohen used to teach us that the first principle of the philosophy of law and government is popular inertia, laziness; and Kafka said that in the end the
only vice was laziness, the mere weight of one's own body.
Nevertheless, in the sexual matter, this has not been my
experience. When—rarely, alas!—there has been absence
of foolish ideas, guilt, fear of the cops, etc., I have found
that "worthwhile" sex is not demanding, complex, and
hard, but precisely cheap, simple, and easy, just as—in
the right conditions of acceptance—making an art-work is
cheap, simple, and easy. (Indeed, it is by analogy with experiences of sex and art that I am a political anarchist: I
hypothesize that if people would get out of their own way
and stop governing themselves, they would have more
peace and justice.) Laziness, like stupidity, is a character-
defense; one must ask what threat of pain or disappoint-
ment makes one's own body a dead weight, rather than
a spring of motion. To be sure, *personal* relations are demanding, complex, jagged, specific—the traits that Donald says I overlook—but it is precisely for these that sex,
in my experience, provides good energy and oil. The natural and general gives us strength for the individual. As St.
Thomas said, a chief use of sex is to know somebody intimately. Some people perversely want to be "understood,"
"loved," "esteemed" before they make love, whereas it is
love-making that leads to understanding, love, and esteem.
Must we not infer that such people regard sex as a betrayal,
insult, or cause of flight (*post coitum tristitia*)?

Similarly, when Donald makes a *dichotomy* between
pornography (and the excited masturbation) and "worthwhile" sexuality, I think he is being excessively strenuous.
The question is not the easy availability and substitute
nature of the pornography and masturbation, but their
quality. Do they entail fear, guilt, and encapsulated fixity?

(E.g. are the images guilty-making? Is the masturbating silent and rigid?) Let us be specific. Much masturbation is escape and consolation in insecurity; much is childlike self-loving, a sexual act *sui generis;* much is a world of temporary withdrawal and daydream; some is without imagery at all. I do not see that any of these—if they are unaccompanied by guilt or humiliation—is incompatible with loving another, or making the effort to find another. Not in my own case or experience. Or we might ask a question of the following type: can a couple tolerate each other's withdrawing into masturbation and still give approving support? This situation would be equivalent either to what Piaget calls the "communal soliloquy" of age 5, or to the accomplice-masturbation of age 10. But these are amiable aspects of life. In America, there is entirely too much preoccupation with being "mature" once and for all; but this prevents continuing growth and a more confident and seasoned maturity.

However—and here I feel I am in agreement with the dominant tone of Donald Phelps' article—all this is much ado about, intellectually, very little. We are discussing the provincial prejudices of a small segment of the Western world during a brief span of its history. These prejudices are important simply because they are empowered, but they are not part of any world that we recognize as making sense. As with racial prejudices or the baroque relics of national states, our chief immediate strategy against them must be to disregard them, when necessary defy them, and defend one another in the consequent troubles. (Our long-range effort, of course, must be to de-energize the causes.)

•

[*In November 1961, I was invited to give a series of three addresses to the Conference of Professional Youth Workers of the Luther League of America. I chose as my subjects* **Prob-**

82 :

*lems of Employment and Vocation, The New De Facto Segre-
gation in Big Northern Cities, and The Responsibility of the
Churches to Change Bad Laws. The following is an edited
tape of the last of these, given on November 8.]*

I'd first like to say something about fear—from a psychological and partly from a theological point of view. . . .

Fear is a very poor means of education: it's a natural
feeling, but isn't educative for the following reason: in
fear there's a shrinking inward from the environment, but
in learning something new the organism has got to go
out to the environment and make a new integration. Fear
prevents integration with the environment. It promotes
adjustment to the environment, but not a creative adjustment.

In emergencies, of course, in order to save the organism
at all, we must have fear and punishment. For example,
an emergency might be that a child goes out into the
street, cars come along, and you grab the child violently
and pull him back. You might then punish him, because
that is a life and death matter which might put the organism out of operation altogether. My bias is that a wise
parent observes very few things that are at that level of
emergency.

The real disadvantage of teaching by fear is that fear
leads to inhibition: one wants to take in the scene spontaneously, but because of remembered punishment holds
back the spontaneous impulse.

I think that this is a loss of innocent faith. Let me illustrate what I mean. When a child runs across the floor in
perfect confidence that the ground is there, he is acting in
faith. Again, if a child asks you a question, in perfectly
sublime faith he expects an answer. With most children
it doesn't take long before you have corrupted their faith
—and I mean *faith* as you people use the word. Children
are born innocent—that is, having faith.

From a psychological point of view this state of faith has perfectly recognizable characteristics: it's spontaneous; it acts with strength; it acts with gracefulness. Kierkegaard said that the man of faith is completely unrecognizable because he acts just like a person, i.e. he really acts very simply.

Clearly, fear and inhibition do injure this faith.

The fear of persons: if one person instills fear in another, then it becomes that much harder for any love to occur.

"The fear of the Lord is the beginning of wisdom."— I would like to read that "the *respect* of the Lord. . . ." By respect I mean regarding the other one as existing, taking the other one seriously as existing. The Lord is not you. He is not something you can use. In that sense, respect for the other person is the beginning of wisdom. It is the beginning of any possible intercourse between the two people.

Apart from fear we learn—with regard to pains, temptations, etc.—by integration. . . .

The soul is an active thing. It takes in and makes new wholes of experience. If the channel between the organism and the environment is left free, then it will integrate new wholes.

For the most part one can trust the self-regulation of the organism to take care of all kinds of matters. That self-regulation is generally known from within, that is, one doesn't teach it.

From this point of view pleasure is a very good indicator of what's good for you: other things being equal, anything that one does that gives pleasure is healthful. This is not to say that pleasure is a criterion for good, but it is a pretty good criterion of a more healthy state as against a neutral or unhealthy state. This is because pleasure is not some accidental thing, but a quality of a completed action with important inner drives operating and a meeting of those impulses from within by opportunities from without. (Of course, it doesn't follow from this that what a person *thinks* will give him pleasure will actually give him pleasure.)

It's an empirical question what the average norms of inner self-regulation are: for example, Luther said that people should have sexual intercourse twice a week. That's an empirical observation—and a rather good one. To me, this seems to be the most beautiful attitude to take toward things like that—that is, this animal can take care of itself, so if we have to give people advice let's see by and large how that animal does operate.

Let me turn to fear in a bigger, political sense—laws which punish and create fear. . . .

Punitive police laws that prohibit people from doing what they want to do not only result in inhibition, but they have a further and much more disastrous result: they tend to aggravate and create anew the very evils that they are supposed to be deterring. I think that the entire history of punitive police legislation has shown this.

Particularly let us talk about narcotics laws and sex laws. . . .

To my mind all of those should be abolished—just forgotten. All of the evils will not vanish, but I think we'll have fewer than now.

It seems to be a propensity of human beings (maybe it's their original sin) that they must find something that's taboo: a survey of the literature of 1890, for example, would show that the horror expressed among religious writers for smoking tobacco was far in excess of anything you'll ever see about marijuana now. In the teens and twenties it was drinking alcohol that was the great taboo.

There's no question that marijuana at present falls into the heading of a taboo. Marijuana is physically and mentally harmless. It has been cleared by the most august of academies of medicine. Yet this harmless indulgence has in the public attitude become "big deal" for a "small deal" thing. What then happens?

The effect of making marijuana illegal is that the price of the stuff goes way up, therefore making it possible for racketeers and criminals to make a good thing out of it. The man who sells you marijuana will see to it—and in the case of boys 15 and 16 years old will see to it success-fully—that his customers become heroin addicts, because there's big money. A dose of pure heroin on an open market (to a physician) runs to about 19¢. Illegal, it goes up to five or ten dollars poor grade. That's a good mark-up! An addict has to have money to have heroin. In the case of a poor Spanish boy in Harlem, he has either to rob to get the money or he becomes a "pusher," getting his fix by getting others on the habit.

What I want to point out is that this is a social problem which has been aggravated because of the law itself.

The actual danger to individuals is not so great. There need not ever have been any emergency attitude with re-gard to it. Heroin is a strong addiction—you are a slave to it—but at the same time it is not especially physically degenerative. It is the practice in some parts of the world —as in England—to regard heroin addiction not in any way as a crime, but as a simple disease. A person who cannot get through the day unless he has a dose of this "medicine," is like a person who has diabetes nad cannot get through the day without a dose of his medicine. Ad-diction is to be treated medically, on prescription, with identification.

But by the law this kind of thing—which is not harm-less, but a serious addiction—has nevertheless been swelled into a vast business with millionaire smugglers and whole networks of pushers, all created because it is a big busi-ness.

J. Edgar Hoover tells us year after year of an increase in crime rate in narcotics and pornography. It seems about time somebody asked the pragmatic question: "Well, if that method you use apparently doesn't work, maybe it's the wrong method."

I think that a better method for dealing with it would be lessening the laws, using other systems which would take these matters completely out of the criminal racket altogether, taking the profits out.

Finally, just a few remarks about sex laws in general. . . .

The chief use of pornography and of the mounting sale of pornography is for young boys (11 and 12 years of age up to 25) to masturbate to. What's wrong with this? Both Dr. Spock and a more liberal manual on child care put out by the Department of Labor agree that with regard to toilet training and masturbation nothing need be done. With regard to masturbation the notion is that this is a normal growth process. If, however, it is forbidden, then it has harmful effects, because it is made guilty and there is a considerable stimulus with inadequate discharge. This is now the opinion of the standard manuals on child care.

The attitude of the parent toward the pornography creates a fear of punishment with regard to the whole sexual act. It's part of an anti-sexual attitude which causes trouble. That is, either the sexual act is natural, innocent, lovely, and learning to engage in it is just part of that whole picture, or it is not. Instead we catch the kids in a sort of trap. If the child doesn't have normal sexual feelings—very wrong. If the child has normal sexual feelings—very wrong. When this happens, the pornography business becomes a good racket.

There are two things which make masturbation harmful: One is if the act is performed wrongly—if the child, for instance, is afraid to make noise as he should during a sexual act. The second is that he feels guilty about the images that he has. But if we combine the attitude of having sex with the attitude of being punished, we get sadistic images.

All of the pornography is full of sadistic images. These are not the normal feelings of an uninhibited child; these are the feelings of an inhibited child brought up in your church. The ones who go in for sadistic literature are the ones brought up in strict Protestant churches. The children brought up permissively and free, if they go in for pornography at all, will like pin-up girls, lovely sexual forms, etc. But the sadistic literature is continually sought out by those who combine the sex which they cannot push away and the feeling that they are being punished. For instance, the audience of Tennessee Williams is the Protestant audience—that is, the combination of lust and punishment.

If you imagine that you're going to turn back the sexual revolution to the time when all of these things were out of mind completely and they could not be discussed as freely as we're discussing them here, you are quite mistaken. Freud pointed out that it is not repression which causes neurosis; it is the breakdown of repression. As long as the entire fabric of society, the habits of people, etc., kept things out of mind, they were just like other things you didn't know anything about. But these things are back in mind; our whole society is largely sexually stimulating (even innocently, with regard to clothes, bathing suits, etc.). As soon as there is that kind of general stimulation in our society, then the repression has vanished. Once the repression has vanished there is no other way to get back to normalcy except to go through the sexual revolution to complete freedom.

What we are now seeing is a considerable freedom

which is not complete freedom, and this leads to the maximum of distortion. And all of the distortions and the perversions are the direct result of the inhibition of what has broken out of repression.

For example, in the TV westerns and crime pictures there is a continual low-grade stimulation without ever discharging. Therefore, you can never be satisfied. Instead of showing the thing in its completion (the cowboy making love to the girl, being sexually excited by her) the sex is never carried to conclusion, but usually cut short by some sort of violence. Why not show the whole thing? That would be salutary to children. It would make them take as a simple fact of life what is a simple fact of life. Instead of sexuality being the whole end of life for children of the ages you treat with (13 to 18), it would become one of the five or six important parts of life—as indeed it is.

As soon as you push sex into the background it begins to pervade all of life.

My opinion on the pornography laws is that you ought to forget them completely. . . .

[*The reception of the religious audience to these talks of mine was mixed. Some were angry that I had been invited, and there was back-stage muttering, reported to me. On the other hand, some who had actual working contact with young people declared that my remarks were common experience and it was time somebody said them out. A couple of people embarrassed me by telling me that I, among them, though a Jew, had most of the spirit of Martin Luther; they were especially moved, I think, by my emphasis on right Vocation in a good community as necessary for a godly life and quite absent from American life.*]

•

[I find no date on the following, but it was written in 1960 after a widely reported conference in New Jersey. The New York Times found no room to print it.]

Editor, *The New York Times*

Dear Sir,

In your interesting story of the debate on doctors' house-calls, Dr. Hudson's insistence on office-calls seemed to have the best of it. I was surprised, however, that the chief uses of family practice went unnoticed, namely, preventive medicine and the diagnosis and treatment of the psychogenic and social factors in illness. A good family physician does not merely "diagnose while a baby brother screamed in the same room," but also has an unofficial look at baby brother. And with regard to the complex but perfectly tangible factors of emotion, diet, hygiene, and environment, it is not the case that one can treat "four or five patients" in an hour. Indeed, the home call gives the physician more information and the family more help quicker and better. Without belittling in any way the use of splendid equipment and an elaborate pharmacopia, it can be said that in treating the whole person and not the symptom, it is often better to settle for the little black bag.

There is a need for both kinds, the specialist (plus the general practitioner in his office) and the family physician. The trouble is that family medicine is not treated *as* a specialty and so taught in the schools, with emphasis on psychosomatic medicine and some training in psychology and social case-work. Such "specialists" would vastly diminish the need for later costly and often ineffective psychotherapy, as well as forestalling some chronic and degenerative diseases. And young men and women with the right disposition for it (certainly the heroes of family practice have a special disposition!) would find this exactly the training that they want for the life they are called to.

Yours,

•

[*A review for the* New York Herald Tribune, *printed October 28, 1962*]

PROBLEMS OF PARENTS, by Benjamin Spock, M.D. (Houghton Mifflin).

Dr. Spock's *Baby and Child Care* (13,000,000 copies) is one of those books, like the old *Boy Scout Handbook,* that admirably fill a social need and have become beneficent institutions. This present book, *Problems of Parents*— with respect to their young and adolescent children—is by the same mind, with most of the same intellectual virtues and much of the same emotional disposition; and yet it is run-of-the-mill, hardly useful, and sometimes pretty base. Why this difference?

Dr. Spock is rare, a philosophical physician. One has no doubt that his science is accurate—he uses his authority with the utmost caution—but he wisely regards medical problems in the context of the whole of on-going life. He makes clear that fussing is not only damaging to persons but might be bad hygiene. And he has an unusually pervasive feeling for relevant psychology, the importance of unconscious motives, the family constellation, the prevalence of reaction-formation and neurotic denial. He does not overlook psychosomatic factors. And he is also a delighted observer of behavior; in the present book, let me single out the fine pages on the three-fold process of learning—trying, doing for its sake, using—for which he gives credit to Myrtle McGraw. His outlook is skeptical but optimistic. All this is present in both *Baby and Child Care* and *Problems of Parents*.

What is famous in the baby book is how these physicianly virtues add up to giving reassurance. Babies are generally tough and will not break, mothers can generally trust their common-sense and natural feelings. Unfortunately, with a remarkable exception to which we must return, Dr. Spock takes a similar tack in the present book and the result is trivial and no better than the *Ladies' Home Journal* for which the essays were written. In my opinion, the difference is this: The purpose of the baby book is to protect the natural development of the growing animals *against* the undue interference and irrational mores of the adults. The babies are tough because they are self-regulating; what they need from the adults is nourishment and affection, which the adults can be trusted to give if they can be themselves. Then the strategy of reassurance works perfectly; it helps the parents let the children be, and it calms them so that they can be themselves.

But in *Problems of Parents* we are mainly dealing not with a self-regulating natural scene, but with a highly conventional society which, bluntly is a bad one, a venal economy, a phony culture, a meretricious standard of living, and a Cold War. Dr. Spock is unhappy about some of this, yet when he now reassuringly advises the parents to affirm their own "high standards," it comes usually to affirming prejudices, conformity, base values, and suburban isolationism. And for the child, "As soon as the adolescent feels convinced that he is an independent adult—when he joins the service, takes a job, marries—then he can stop complaining about his parents and begin, happily, to behave very much like them." What job? what service? In my opinion, this is a betrayal of the young, and of the possibility of a future for America.

Unlike the baby book, *Problems of Parents* suffers from

a monstrous middle-classness. It is peppered with phrases like "Every established family has—" But these parents do not deserve reassurance, but a shock. In fact, their growing children are increasingly giving them the shock, and are miserable themselves, but one would have little sense of this from Dr. Spock. In 300 pages there is no mention of drug-taking, of serious sexual difficulties or deviations, of delinquency, of kids in jail for noble causes, of youth-unemployment, of urban poverty. Maybe it will be said that he is not writing for families like that; my guess is that, one way or another, there are very few families that are not "like that."

To Dr. Spock, hard cases admittedly exist, but his uniform advice for coping with them is, astoundingly, to seek help from a psychiatrist, a child guidance clinic, a family social agency. This refrain, which recurs again and again, is of course the opposite of the self-reliance that inspirited the baby book, and it is disastrous to reassurance. Maybe it is wise advice, but its meaning is that the adults too are not taken seriously. When the chips are down, modern life is too complicated for them; it is no use even trying to explain it to them in the *Ladies' Home Journal*. But the professionals and administrators can apparently take over better. Consider the following: "If the dread of going to school is intense and persistent, the parent should promptly get in touch with a child psychiatrist." Maybe so; but the doctor does not equally suggest that the parent might wisely clamor at the School Board. Why in such a case Dr. Spock assumes that the child is crazy is quite beyond me. I am on a School Board myself.

Typical of Dr. Spock's lack of perception of what is at stake is his handling of the TV-watching. He is unhappy about the crime and violence; he understands that the case that they are dangerous has not been proved; but he says that they "may lower the children's standards and give them a poor impression of humanity." It does not strike him that, far worse and obviously character-forming, is the clown mouthing the commercial, because this image is accepted as an approved sample of humanity.

Let me put my point another way. Dr. Spock's title is erroneous. There are no problems of parents as parents; the problems are of the grown-ups as people in the society they are responsible for, and in which children cannot reasonably grow up. Contrast this title with one of A. S. Neill's, the progressive educator, *The Problem Parent*. For Neill, consistently, the parents are failing as persons and the kids must still be protected against them rather than brought to conform to them.

By the time he gets to the end of these articles, Dr. Spock is also disturbed. He is strongly concerned about the bomb-testing and the threat of total destruction facing us. And in this book, as in his public life, he stands up for his own values. Suddenly his tone is entirely different. It is a responsible advocacy for what he holds to be prudent and just, with objective arguments. There is no more recourse to clinics or psychologizing about a secure structure no matter what the structure. What Dr. Spock does not understand in his bones is how the Cold War is intimately and essentially related to the kind of lives that his parents are leading, the TV they watch, the schools they provide, the jobs they work at.

4

LAPSE OF COMMUNITY

•

November 13, 1959

The Honorable F. Wagner
Mayor of New York City

Dear Sir,
   Every night your voice comes over the radio declaring
that the parents of children not yet at home ought to "evaluate their responsibilities as parents."
   A teen-ager who has not yet returned to the one room
inhabited by his parents and perhaps three other children, while you allow Robert Moses still to sit in office,
might well say, "It is time for you to evaluate your
responsibilities as Mayor."

                                        Yours truly,

cc: *New York Post*

   [*No answer.*]

•

July 15, 1960
Editor, *New York Herald Tribune*

Dear Sir,

When Robert Moses criticizes as "impulsive" Newbold Morris's complaint about the exclusion of our city boys from Westchester swimming pools, he is conveniently overlooking some perfectly obvious facts. The exurbanites of the near counties get their income in our city; they enjoy its cultural opportunities paid for by our city; they daily and nightly use our city services and clutter up our streets with their persons and cars. They then, legally but inequitably, avoid our city sales taxes by buying in our great stores and using ex-urban addresses. And worst of all, they are enabled to carry on this dual life by the system of voraciously expanding highways that are used in vast disproportion by their commutation, but are paid for more equally by the citizens of the state as a whole. It has not been the primary necessity or convenience of the people of New York City to pour so much of our public money into these landscaped roads, rather than into the housing, schools, and community planning that we do need.

In such circumstances, it is galling to see underprivileged kids from the city, who travel by subway and bus, turned away from a pool in Westchester.

Mr. Moses won himself a reputation as a man who "got things done." So he did; but they were usually the wrong things. Now we have the task of undoing some of the damage that he did our city over many years. Let us encourage Mr. Morris to some more "impulsiveness."

Yours,

cc: Newbold Morris

[*Not printed.*]

•

[On the same day I seem to have written the following. James Wechsler is the Editor of the New York Post, *personally unknown to me. "Kessler" refers to an architect involved in a miserable Urban Renewal gouge, on a Webb and Knapp project, resulting in his being forbidden by Mayor Wagner to do any further public work in New York City. His name reappeared as one of the architects for the Webb and Knapp portion of the Lincoln Square Urban Renewal.]*

July 15, 1960

Dear James Wechsler,

I don't remember that we've ever met. I'm sorry to have had to be so rough in reviewing your recent book (*New Leader*), but I always call them as I see them. But I think you've done good things with the paper. I'm especially concerned, as you perhaps know, with city planning and I want to make the city better. Maybe you can use me or we can use each other. (I don't want a job. I do have lots of time for concrete proposal and concrete action that I believe in.)

Let me say what prompts this advance on my part. That convention in Los Angeles. The spectacle of the New York delegation shamefully misrepresenting the N.Y. public. This made me so dejected that I now react to it with a positive counter-attack; it's what Riesman calls my nerve of failure.

A couple of things occur to me at the moment. Newbold Morris's timid remarks about the Westchester swimming pools must be pushed all the way. Those bastards get their income here, use our facilities and museums, clutter up the streets with their cars. Then they avoid our sales taxes with their exurban addresses. But worst of all, Moses poured all that money into parkways used disproportionately by their commutation, whereas we in the city patently have needed quite different public services. (This is what's wrong with Galbraith. He doesn't think of "public goods" concretely, in terms of what they really do.) Again, we must not let drop the business of Lincoln Square, e.g. the employment of Kessler. My brother is the professor of Community Planning at Columbia, and I think we could mount a mass meeting of students and perhaps a few days' picketing on that kind of outrage. It would certainly do the University some good. If those faculties are not responsible for the kind of city we have, who in hell is?

One thinks of one example after another. The *Post* has "covered" plenty of them. But what I'm after is this: not merely to have "coverage"—which in the end can result only in cynicism and the sense that "nothing can be done." This is the Achilles heel of liberal journalism. What must be added is the persisting insistence on each concrete particular case, unwilling to rest until satisfaction is given. Confronting the individual involved, and insisting on the existent fact. This is the only way to crack the organization. How to do this? Why can't we talk it over for a couple of hours?

Sincerely,

[*Mr. Wechsler chose not to acknowledge this letter.*]

•

[*I was astonished to be asked by the* Harvard Educational Review *to review James Conant's latest book, for Dr. Conant had been President of Harvard and I have notoriously been no friend of Dr. Conant's on education. When I wryly submitted this review, for Spring 1962, I asked if it was what they expected. I received the reply that it was what they had "hoped for." I cannot explain this further than to say that perhaps a new day is dawning.*]

SLUMS AND SUBURBS, James B. Conant. McGraw-Hill, New York, 1961.

In his visits to the city neighborhoods and schools throughout the country, Dr. Conant was frequently "jolted" and "disturbed" by the conditions that he met with, and he has "sought to create a set of anxious thoughts in the minds of the conscientious citizens who, living in the suburbs, may work in the city." After reading *Slums and Suburbs,* one cannot avoid the question how, in the first place, a man was ever chosen to survey the schools who is so unfitted by his own experience, training and type of mind. He could certainly have seen these conditions not far from Harvard. One is struck by his technological and even economic approach, as if the pragmatic problem to be solved were the allocation of resources, rather than the psychological and political one of renewing society with each growing generation. Naturally, in the post-Sputnik delirium, our Establishment would choose a Scientist and an Administrator. Having little acquaintance with social or psychological reality, and being apparently quite complacent with the dominant goals of our Nation, Dr. Conant often expresses his "impatience" with "hair-splitting" philosophers and their educational ideals. His own philosophy has been that the purpose of schooling is simply to man the Cold War and train technicians and semi-skilled apprentices for the corporations and other businesses as usual. In this new book, however, he discovers that we must also watch out for the "social dynamite" of accumulated frustration and resentment among those who are out-caste in the present dispensation; yet again his concern is to regularize things, rather than to improve the electorate, the proper educational aim of a democracy. I have grown impatient with Dr. Conant. In this short review of a short book, let me pass by his characteristic virtues of eartnestness and moderation, and concentrate on the shortcomings of his sociology and pedagogy.

Dr. Conant discusses mainly the northern Negro slums where the schools are increasingly *de facto* segregated and are very inadequate. At considerable length he belittles stratagems of integration; for instance, open enrollment allowing children to be sent out of the neighborhood to better white schools. A chief argument that he uses is, curiously, the arid legalism that *Brown et al vs. Topeka* forbids segregation on color grounds *solely*, whereas the present segregation is because of neighborhood plan and housing, and not because of color! So the scientific mind. But of course the exact point of *Brown* was that color, socio-economic, and community segregation is one integral social fact preventing equality of opportunity, and to the child is one inseparable psychological whole. The honorable and logical next step, in the face of *de facto* segregation, must be to try to get rid of housing and income segregation. But this, says Dr. Conant, is quite "impossible"—it is hard but not impossible—and to insist that white and Negro children be mixed in the classroom is, according to Dr. Conant, "extremely defeatist." Indeed, with his general tendency to achieve the *immediate* maximum-efficient allocation of resources for non-educational purposes, Dr. Conant must consider the mixture of slums and suburbs *un*desirable, for it would dilute the high I.Q.'s. (His ideal school, as explained in this book, is the "challenging" Bronx High School of Science, although he does not mention that BHSS is segregated at least 75% Jewish, the bright children of ambitious and often poor parents chosen from the vast population of Manhattan and the Bronx, with plenty of "open enrollment.") Instead, Dr. Conant's solution for the inadequate Negro schools is to spend more money and make them equal in plant and staff to the suburban schools; that is, he returns to *Plessy vs. Ferguson,* equal but separate facilities, as if the Warren court had not spoken at all! It is not by such reasoning that he will dampen the social dynamite; he affirms just what the fight is about. His belief that a kind of integration can be achieved by having a mixed *staff* quite overlooks the Uncle Tom effect of such paternalism, for what the child learns is that "all whites are persons in authority; some Negroes can become teachers too, just like whites."

Open enrollment *is* a poor expedient. The few whites rapidly disappear and only the better-off Negro parents can afford or care to use the opportunity, so that color and income-segregation increases. Commutation is always to be avoided if possible, and certainly small children should not be twice-daily boarding buses. Among our excessively mobile population, neighborhood attachment should be strengthened rather than weakened, especially the attachment of the less out-caste. Nevertheless, as psychological encouragement and as simple justice, I do not see any other interim possibility than to allow this choice.

Our social policy, however, must be not to improve the slum schools as such, but *to get rid of the suburbs*—physically if possible, but at least as a separate and separatist way of life. We must reverse our public policy on F.H.A. loans, which has encouraged the automobiles, the payment of sales-taxes at the point of delivery, etc., and use the accruing money to improve the *urban* neighborhoods; thereby we shall integrate and improve the schools. Dr. Conant treats the suburbs as if they were a long-established condition deeply engrained in social nature; he does not seem to realize that the suburban flight has been an artifact of class-legislation spending billions of the public-money for escape-roads and real-estate and tax advantages, that should have gone to making a good city. Conversely, when he coyly (and truly) derides the pedagogic relevance of better heating and plumbing in urban housing, he astonishingly does not seem to know the newsy fact that our public housing, the work of fools, grafters, and profiteers, has uprooted neighborhoods, built in income-segregation as a principle, driven out enterprises useful to the communities, created delinquency, and usually not bothered if there is a school at all. It is not heating and plumbing that have pedagogic relevance, but the quality of the environment and the doings of the families that choose to live in that environment. Under these circumstances, it is by no means so absurd as Dr. Conant thinks to try the other tack for a while; to try, devilishly, to district or bus so that middle-class children have to go to slum schools. This would, very speedily and realistically, improve those schools and begin to improve and integrate those neighborhoods—we know how the white parents squawk at even the open-enrollment. (I quote the President of a Junior High P.T.A: "It is a mistake to transport children from far away; the morale of our school is being destroyed by overcrowding.") On the other hand, appeals to conscientious anxiety will get nowhere—from the history of P.S. 119 in New York, one is not impressed by the celerity with which the present regime exterminates rats from slum schools.

Dr. Conant's bent of mind leads him to a persistent embarrassment in logic. On the one hand, he is quite sure that a correct allocation of abilities to different life-careers, academic or "vocational," college or post-graduate, can be predetermined by tests. "How can aptitude be determined? By noting the judgment of the teachers, and by considering the scores on scholastic aptitude and intelligence tests . . . to make rough predictions of future success." (He apparently does not know Getzels and Jackson on the unreliability of teachers' judgments and tests for even aca-

demic achievement; and what would he make of the conclusion of Bruner and his colleagues—or, for that matter,
of Freud—that this kind of grading might be *destructive*
of real achievement?) On the other hand, he understands
that the low scoring in the slums is perhaps *entirely* due
to background conditions. He mentions the "startling im-
provements on test scores" in the Higher Horizons program (of Dan Schreiber), which is aimed at orienting underprivileged children toward college in spite of social
obstacles; and he speaks of the "astonishing results" of the
Banneker program, which relates community and school
and forgets the scores altogether, in the manner of old-
fashioned progressive education. Given this contradiction
between strong reliance on the tests and the perhaps entire
irrelevance of the tests, one would assume that, to conserve
human resources and elevate the population, an educator
would lay his main stress on changing social conditions
and *vastly* increasing the pool of talent. Even technologi-
cally, this would, apparently rather quickly, pay off, if the
reforms were deep and thoroughgoing. But quite to the
contrary, Dr. Conant speedily settles for a "vocational"
program for the low-scorers (I put the word in quotation-
marks since it pains me to see this beautiful notion, of
finding a child's true vocation or calling, debased to the
usual meaning and practice.) His problem is then to get
the trained children into existing jobs in the community,
and to tailor the training *toward* those jobs. He does not
entertain the idea that perhaps it is partly *because* of the
very prospect of those jobs and the lack of incentive to fit
into that existing community, that there are so many low-
scorers, and drop-outs 75% unemployed, and high-school
graduates 50% unemployed. He does not criticize the jobs,
he hardly considers the structure of the community, he is
clear only about the "social" goals. Whose goals? The

success of all programs like Higher Horizons comes from taking the children seriously as human beings, with sentiments and purposes that make up a whole existence.

In the suburbs where the majority will go on to college, Dr. Conant, in the interests of efficiency, finds that he must again separate the sheep from the goats; for many who are college-bound because of money or family ambitions, are not really academically talented enough to go on to graduate and professional work. (Incidentally, the magic ratio of the academically talented was, nationally, "15%" in 1959, but now, curiously, it is "15-20%".) The less gifted must not aim for the "prestige colleges"—Dr. Conant uses the expression without quotation marks—whose chief function is to service professional and graduate schools (although, incidentally again, the director of admissions at Harvard informs me that it is "phony" to go to Harvard just to advance up the ladder, and he disapproves of a youngster "doing" a high-school just to "make" a college.) Now how, in the suburbs, does the competitive selectivity of Dr. Conant work out in actuality? Dr. Conant is disturbed that many suburban children, pushed by ambitious parents, break down in trying to overachieve; and, with admirable class-loyalty, he solemnly, in italics, assures the parents that there are other, less prestigious colleges available for the less gifted who have money. But I can assure him that suburban adolescents have their own devices to protect themselves from breakdown. For instance, since grading is on the bell-curve, those who might perform too well and make it hard for everybody, agree, or are persuaded, to restrain their ability, just as adult factory workers have a code to produce neither too much nor too little. (James Coleman of Johns Hopkins has, in *The Adolescent Society*, given us a study of many such "constraints against being a good student.") Conversely, at schools like Bronx Science—I am a Bronx Science parent—the rate of cheating, as reported in the school paper last spring, goes as high as 70% in the senior year, though it is only 25% in the freshman year. This makes excellent training to end up as a Westinghouse or General Electric executive in jail, but it does not have direct relevance to the habit of science. Let me quote also from an editorial in the student paper of the Harvard Business School, that people are "placed by society and the pressure of capitalist conformity in a position where they can succeed only by violating the laws." Thus, among hip kids, the very devices of selection, grading, and competitiveness that our author relies on to produce competence, are likely to produce either sabotage or crime.

Though he speaks of a "general or liberal" education, Dr. Conant seems to have no concept of a liberal education at all. His purpose is always teleological, whereas the purpose of a liberal education is to bring up the young to be new centers of initiative and citizenly responsibility. He explains the reason for general education in the following odd sentence: "Talented students should develop specific skills in high school that, if not developed, restrict their choice of careers." That is, we do not want to educate free men who might take over, but adaptable kits of marketable skills. The "vocational" training for the lower I.Q.'s, effectually for the vast majority of the underprivileged class, is aimed toward specific opportunities in the neighborhoods, to give each child a single marketable skill, an apprentice-system at the public expense; but how will this educate a nation?

On the upward ladder, no age growth seems to have needs of its own; everything is oriented to the future. For instance, Dr. Conant considers the junior-high idea as indifferent, so long as the "program" is right. One would have thought that the program and method would be importantly determined by the transition into puberty—but to be sure, since the sexual has been banned from the junior high as from the rest of the school system, Dr. Conant is right, the idea *is* indifferent. At the upper end of the ladder, correspondingly, the quicker the specific adaptation to the career, the better—according to Dr. Conant the advantages of 3 years of under-graduate college rather than 4 "hardly need be emphasized." And up the whole ladder, finally, "the ideal situation, in the best interests of both the individual and society," is the smooth transition throughout, and the immediate placement of the graduate by the job-bureau of the university; he singles out Engineering as the best example. (It is extraordinary, if this is so ideal, how the youth of the more sophisticated East are choosing *away* from this good example.) That is, we are to make professionals who know nothing, who have been speeded up, who have explored nowhere, who have not had a chance to mature even psychosexually. It is this monstrous doctrine and practice that have already long saddled us with an inhumane and uncitizenly society, with slums of engineering without community-plan, with unphilosophical medicine, a useless and venal technology, a sheepish electorate, a debased culture and jejune teachers who cannot relate the tradition and the world, and politics like Dr. Conant's. This is the education of the Organization. There is nothing newly threatening in any of Dr. Conant's books, nothing to be up in arms about; he strides the middle of the established road; it is a disaster.

The relation of society and school is necessarily ambiguous. Society demands the school it thinks it needs, and for the most part it gets what it deserves. Yet the school also has its own aims and as a community of youth and of concernful and somewhat detached and idealistic adults, it continually offers a possibility of change and growth. A wise society protects this cambium, this growing layer.

The dialectic of this perennial ambiguity is the philosophy of education, with which Dr. Conant is so impatient. Dr. Conant does not conceive himself as a philosopher but as a kind of social-engineer, primarily to provide personnel and training, secondarily to avoid trouble. But man being what he is, I doubt that it is possible to get adequate personnel or avoid trouble unless one has higher aims than Dr. Conant. He is entirely impractical, for by the time some of these kids grow up, the world, if there is a world, will look very different.

•

[*This is a letter on a review of my* Utopian Essays *and Practical Proposals, sometime in 1961. I wrote it when just back from a conference at West Point on Mental Health in Manhattan, where it was agreed by all the conferees that our social services had to be much more tailor-made to do any good.*]

Editor, *The Morningsider*
New York,

Dear Sir,
    Let me thank E. B. Koren for his friendly review of my new book. I am not sure, however, what he means by his final critical remark and I think it is worth exploring publicly. He says that my "proposals seem incapable of dealing with the magnitude of current dilemmas" to which I give "such consistently clear analysis."
    If this means that I do not cover the field, I strongly agree. What we need is *many* people who pay close attention and exercise their wills toward simplifying situations and, finally, inventing solutions to the causes of our difficulties. One reason for my writing such a book of practical proposals is to hearten others and put a bug in their minds.
    If my critic means that my proposals are too weak for

the particular problems I apply them to, I disagree. Manhattan *can* be made more livable, our neighborhoods *can* be improved, by banning the non-service automobiles. Growing up *can* be immensely aided by the general institution of youth work-camps with a variety of rural and urban projects thought up by young professionals and not bureaucrats. Etc.

But I fear—and this is why I am writing this letter—that my critic has a tendency to look always for large-scale solutions to our multifarious problems, and this is the very attitude that, in my opinion, causes our troubles. It is the way of liberals to try to solve a problem by pasting it on the wall and throwing a lot of money at it. But very many stubborn and terrible problems can be solved only by particular and tailor-made application to themselves. Every settlement house knows this; the attempt to centralize such houses, to work out "general principles" of settlement work, and to have "professional standards" of personnel, etc. is ruinous. It leads to dilution and irrelevance. This is what has happened, for instance, to the Higher Horizons program that Dan Schreiber developed so brilliantly on a shoe-string grant for his own school, where he knew the particular cases to work with. But alas! it is far easier to get a million dollars for a "large scale" attack on a "problem" than to get a number of tiny grants for many concrete situations.

Yours,

●

[*In* Liberation, *August, 1961.*]

The New York Times of June 4 contained one of its frequent special advertising supplements devoted to the industry and tourism of a nation of the world. This one was "sponsored and the material prepared by South African and American business interests as a guide to South Africa." Because of the racial policy of the Union of South Africa, there is a melancholy interest in describing this document.

Its principle is explained in the foreword statement, "Workshop of a Continent," in the following paragraphs:

"Dr. Ernest Dichter, president of the Institute of Motivational Research, makes the point that even the average American tourist in Johannesburg looks at fact-filled pamphlets publicizing the country and says to himself mentally: 'I know you're trying to pull the wool over my eyes. You're trying to tell me that things in this country aren't too bad—well, who are you kidding? I know what goes on here.' He has rejected the facts rather than change his mind.

"Dr. Dichter suggests that information on South Africa should read something like this: 'So you've heard that in this country we have *apartheid*, a police state, slave labor, etc., well, we'd like to tell you a few other things.' "

Dr. Dichter has explained to me at length that science, including his psychological science, is purely neutral and objective and can be applied to a good or bad cause. I presume that he was amply rewarded for his advice to this bad cause.

Let us turn to this fact-filled pamphlet. It contains 35 photographs showing human beings; four of these show Negroes. The actual white population of South Africa is less than 20%.

One photo showing a Negro is the cover. It is a busy scene of traders on the floor of the Johannesburg Stock Exchange; on the balcony is a young Negro marker alertly waiting to chalk the figures.

The other three figures are part of a two-page spread

of 22 photos called "Take a Tour of South Africa." There are whites fishing, working in a mine, surf-riding, bus-drivers conversing, shopping, father-and-daughter, a comic behind, a pin-up girl, merchant mariners drinking, dining. The photos of Negroes are: cute five-year-olds singing; two youths playing "penny whistles"; and a merry fat mammy balancing a valise on her head and perched on the handle-bars of a bicycle pushed by a spooky-eyed coon.

It is appalling that this kind of stereotyped garbage can still be printed, and paid for by Americans (and passed by Dr. Dichter?). In this magazine no Negro is shown working. The whites must work terribly hard, in that Workshop of a Continent, to support a colored population more than four times their own.

On page seven, in parallel columns, with photographs, are statements by C. R. Swart, the South African Minister of Justice, and John F. Kennedy. Mr. Swart's statement starts by pointing out the similarity of the pioneer settlement of South Africa and the United States. (On another page is a drawing of a covered wagon being attacked by savages.) He ends with the remark that "South Africa and the United States have mutual interests in defense strategy and are cooperating extensively in space research. Slowly people are beginning to realize that the Republic of South Africa is not a stretch of steaming jungle, but rather a modern Western nation, vital and highly civilized, differing from the Republic of the United States basically only in size."

Cheek by jowl with this, the face of President Kennedy tells us:

> [Africa] "is a land of immense importance to the world and to the United States. Some may look at it from the viewpoint of the vital natural resources and strategic materials. Some may be interested in military bases or new allies against Communism. Some may feel a responsi-

bility in Africa because the West thrust itself upon the area and cannot be indifferent to the consequences. Some may have a real concern for Africa and her people. But whatever one's point of view, one fact cannot be denied —the future of Africa will seriously affect, for better or worse, the future of the United States."

The colossal moral stupidity with which the President of the United States here regards ordinary human concern as one possible "viewpoint" among several—which one may or may not have—must not pass unnoticed. And in this context! This is the fellow who dares to urge our young people into a Peace Corps for service.

Most of the products advertised are industrial. The only ones that seem subject to boycott by ordinary consumers are travel and South African Rock Lobster Tails.

•

[*In* Dissent, *Spring, 1957.*]

SEGREGATION, THE INNER CONFLICT IN THE SOUTH, by Robert Penn Warren. (Random House)

The publisher's wrapper speaks of this little book as a "sympathetic, fair, and honest report." And so it is. Yet it is disingenuous and not disinterested, and it is a conceited little book. What it says sheds no light, but its way of saying it happens to be an excellent brief example of a kind of southern literary attitude, and it is worth discussing; especially since this attitude dovetails neatly into the conceit and disingenuousness (much closer to dishonesty) of *Life* magazine for which the reportage was made. Penn Warren's disingenuousness is this: he sees, he cannot help but see, that the Negro problem in the south is a psychiatric one, a matter of irrational emotions and split identity; all the usual reasons are largely rationalizations; and indeed he subtitles his book "inner conflict," a term picked up from psychoanalysis. Yet the author persists in striking the postures and sounding the rhetoric of being in an agonizing moral dilemma, as if a problem of medicine were a problem of ethics. This is a spurious seriousness, a confusion, as Aristotle would have said, between the tragic and the merely pathetic. To be sure, no one likes to be looked at as sick and "merely pathetic," and he puts it to himself otherwise, but that putting is conceit.

Let me ask the reader to imagine himself back in 1850 and the Fugitive Slave Law, and to compare that situation with our present one following the Supreme Court's decisions against segregation. In 1850, the Law, written in the Constitution itself and strongly affirmed by the Court, offended many a northern heart and soul. The northerners nullified the law and ran their undergrounds; now the southerners are nullifying the law and have their mobs. In both cases, a direct clash between popular sentiment and law; and generally in such cases the law must finally give way. Yet there is a crucial difference between these two nullifications (and there is an unanimous informed opinion that the southern popular sentiment will give way, it will not make law).

In 1850 the man whose sentiment made him shelter the runaway and defy the law, felt himself fortified by all ethics, fairness, the golden rule, the spirit of the Constitution and the Declaration, Christian, deist, or transcendental metaphysics—all these were on the side of his sentiment; and if he would be punished for his lawless act, he would be judged as a decent man or a martyr, depending on his enthusiasm. But the southerner who cannot stomach the black boy in the school is precisely inwardly betrayed by most of these same ideals and conscientious considerations; he only feels he is in the right, he rather knows he is in the wrong; and it takes a lot of loud shouting and banding together to feel right enough to act in such a case. (It is the difference between a lynch mob and personal moral conviction.) That is, the stronger law and the better reason are on one side; and on the other are only passions, and reasons of the blood, the gorge, and the jealous nightmare.

Now if such passions opposed to the ideal and beginning to lose the sanction of conventional authority, nevertheless cannot be downed in a man and even break into overt action, then that man is going to be very sick. He is certainly an object of physicianly compassion (probably a more practical proposition than "a case for the police"). But he is not, as such, an object for tragic pity, for brooding with like Hamlet, or of whom to say, as this author does, that he has a "moral problem."

Penn Warren understands perfectly that fundamentally we have to do with unassimilable and self-disintegrating sentiments. "The reality is the fact of self-division." Reporting his informal interviews and asking his question, "What are the reasons for segregation?" he collects a list of responses: "Pridefulness (here meaning, you gotta be better than somebody), money (for instance, wage differentials), level of intelligence, race (miscegenation), filth and disease, power, hate, contempt, legality." He himself lays a personal stress on one other factor, "piety," in the sense of sticking to grandfather's ways. But in the end, none of these seems to him to be the essential thing; rather, "the problem is to learn to live with ourselves. . . . Desegregation will come when enough people in a particular place cannot live with themselves any more"; and he climaxes this passage with an excellent example of a person not able to live with herself; a crazy old lady who hears non-existent voices of Negroes screaming in the night, being burned alive.

This makes sense, a disordered personality, a psychiatric case. And I guess it is the feeling that people who are not sick in this particular way experience when we meet with people who are crazy in this way, whether in New York or in New Orleans. But what is remarkable now is that Penn Warren by no means goes on from this line of reasoning, to ask, for instance, the pertinent psychological questions, to ask for dreams and sexual fantasies, to notice the relevant character symptoms and obsessional defenses against anxiety, to explore (what is striking) the likeness of delusional jealousy. Quite the contrary! He suddenly takes a moral stance of exhortation to the good way. Does he really think that the crazy old lady of his image will be helped by that kind of talk? If he thinks so, he's a fool; if he means his image to be taken less earnestly, he's a lousier writer than he is.

Let me put it another way: If you examine the list of "reasons" quoted above, that the reporter is satisfied with having collected, you find that it is altogether blank with respect to the standard contemporary theory of Prejudice (and certainly we are deailng with cases of prejudice). In the center of a standard analysis would be the notion of "reaction-formation"; that the prejudice is a means of bolstering the repression of the inacceptable parts of oneself ("one's own ape-like nature", the southerner's wishful suspicion that he is a nigger); and the prejudice allows the consequent projections to alleviate tension, and spiteful aggressions to win small victories. Whatever the merits of this contemporary theory—it has great merits—it is simply the bread-and-butter of any attempt to describe the kind of behavior we read from Clinton, Tennessee; and all of the other reasons readily group themselves in such a theory, both as causes and effects. Surely a Pulitzer Prize winner has heard of such things. I have no novel information on this subject-matter and I do not intend to spin again these well-spun speculations; but I want simply to ask the question, how is it conceivable that this sophisticated author proceeds as if no such further avenues of analysis existed?

The question is an important one; for when, on the contrary, he pursues his analysis to the point of split identity and then suddenly jumps to ethics and justice—"one small episode in the long effort for justice"—then he does no good and some harm; he creates an impasse and bypasses the present. If it is an ethical problem (or ·a fortiori a political problem), one must address it with present indignation, determination, sacrificial love, enthusiasm, organization, or however one has the will and skill. None of this is in Penn Warren's little book. If it is a medical problem, one goes on to employ or indicate or at least suggest the not brilliant but by no means empty armamentarium of social psychiatry. None of this is in Penn Warren's little book. But the effect of what he does—I do not think it is his intention—is to stall the works. This is to be disingenuous, for he must have both more live impulses and better sense. He seems to want to cry out "Help! help us!" but instead he stalks off (or drowns) in his dignity.

This brings us back, I guess, to the conceit of a little southern book like this. By "conceit" let us here mean a fantastic concept of oneself that one clings to for fear of an intolerable feeling of emptiness or defeat if it is given up. In the present case there are two strands, the southern conceit, which is merely a bit trying (still fighting the Civil War), and the more virulent conceit of *Life* magazine, which is a pain in the ass.

If we consider the author's handling of his list of reported reasons, he seems to warm to two: the kind of false pride that says, "They can't push me around," without having an idea to give true courage in Socrates' sense; and especially piety, in the sense of loyalty to our history.

Now "history" is of course a big deal with southern writers ("he is a man of character and force . . . of fine intelligence . . . he reads Roman history"). But let us look at the following remark of Penn Warren's. He is describing a 15-year-old who has come to inspect an old fort in Nashville; the boy is portrayed as particularly attractive, appealing, and manly—until suddenly he shies away with ugly suspicious anger because the reporter doesn't share his hatred for nigger-bastards. The author remarks, "And somehow the hallowedness of the ground he stood on had vindicated, as it were, that hate." What the devil does that sentence mean? If he means to say that there is an intrinsic connection between the history and its present-day consequences, and the consequences are admittedly ugly and unfortunate, then how is the ground "hallowed"? Would it not be wiser sadly to reassess the history, rather than to become pompous? Certainly the scene of any past epic or tragic event must evoke thought and even passionate concern and pride for ourselves if there is ground for pride; but it is not hallowed, not hallowed unless the outcome is holy.

I am reminded of the tone of, say, C. G. Bowers' *The Tragic Era*, where he lauds the beauty and virtue and learning and mores of his *ante-bellum* heroes, and he deplores with anguished sentimentality the evil days that have come and the offended womanhood, but never does he ask whether the infatuations of the former did not produce the latter (as the infatuations of the north have produced their own catastrophes, but nobody would boast of it.) Penn Warren does not, of course, try to defend the southern culture, nor to suggest that there is any present culture to save; but he does tend to make past tragedies a bulwark of present conceit.

In the same vein, he dwells a lot on the reasons springing from a defense of regionalism—resistance to the centralized constitution and the sociologists. But for heaven's sake, he is writing for *Life* magazine! that organ of decentralized integral culture! A regionalism that defends its peculiar and unprofitable excellences is an honorable thing, and a regionalism that can make them exemplary and viable, is a wonderful thing; but a regionalism that is jealous of its *right* to segregate, is conceit, a defense against being swallowed up by one's stupid betters. Let me put it another way: in the present economy and culture, almost the only earmark of the South *as* a region is the segregation; and if that's the case, forget it and draw the line elsewhere.

Finally, I must, although it is boring, mention the specific conceit of style that is germane to writing for Luce publications. This occurs when there is an "objective" and "impartial" reporting of what cannot possibly be manfully confronted without indignation or grief or love or compassion or such. Then the resulting woeful emptiness is concealed by dramatizing the self-conceited reporter or photographer. There are tricks of rhythm and tricks of ordering.

For instance, the terse bang-bang isolated concluding sentence: "... A girl from Mississippi had said to me, etc. *Paragraph.* I know what she meant. *End of Section.*" "He asks me if I have been talking to a lot of people. *Paragraph.* I had been talking to a lot of people. *End of Section.*" "I had said it for a joke. *Paragraph.* But had I? *End of Section.*" (This is really too vulgar.)

An alternative ending is the irrelevant long-rhythmed picturesque fadeout, as: "*Paragraph.* I look down the interminable row of dingy houses, over the interminable flat of black earth toward the river. *End of Section.*" "*Paragraph.* It is late afternoon. I hear the pullulation of life, the stir and new tempo toward evening, the babble of voices, a snatch of laughter. I hear the remorseless juke boxes. They shake the air. *End of Section.*"

Or again, he makes use of the snap-to-attention italicized repetitions, punctuating a factitious on-and-on flow: "*What's coming?* 'Whatever it is,' the college student says . . . *What's coming?* And the Methodist minister . . . *What's coming?* I ask the handsome, big . . . *What's coming?* And the college student says . . . *What's coming?* And a state-official says . . . *What's coming?* And a man in Arkansas says . . ." (The movies have much to answer for!)

There is no use in multiplying types and examples; any page of *Life* is a lead-mine for a prospector. Given these mannerisms it is obviously impossible to say a serious word; but my point is that the manner is not the cause but the result of the sterile attitude adopted. Like any other conceit, however, it does create a false security in the writer and publisher (and presumably in some readers) that something is going on.

More direct in method is the conceit of the "impartial reporter," given by impartially skipping from one immediate close-up to another. In this little report impartiality means that approximately equal space is given to white and black: the white close-ups and black close-ups are mixed as if at random; there are sympathetic specimens of each; and bad marks are scored against both.

Frankly, if desegregation is a matter of justice, as the author says on his next to the last page, I find it hard to understand what he thinks he is doing by this mode of scoring; is not impartiality the virtue of a referee in an equal competition with strict rules? But more generally, in this kind of reportage there is a confusion between impartiality and disinterestedness. Disinterestedness is non-attachment to one's particular interests and concentration on the truth of the case; it therefore often eventuates in a passionate advocacy of a new something. Of this beautiful intellectual virtue there is very little in *Life* magazine and not much in Penn Warren's *Segregation.* "Impartial reporting" of the kind here is a conceited attitude to protect the writer and reader from experience, and to substitute conversation-pieces.

•

[To A. J. Muste, on my being asked to sponsor a pro-integration pamphlet about which I had reservations. Probably in 1960.]

Dear A.J.,

I'm a little disturbed by the pamphlet. The bulk of it, on the south, is first-rate, vigorous and interesting. But does the section on the national and international scene make much sense? He seems to rely on a majority in the Democratic party—e.g. organized labor—that willingly takes Kennedy and Johnson; and is there any evidence whatever that it is not positively *for* the armaments? As Kahn knows, of course, the background of the southern change has been the industrial and international necessity: from *that* point of view desegregation is just an incident, to get rid of an impediment to the American century. But the vital part has been the negro's and white's needs as human beings in the south, their clash and mutual benefit.

I'd be pleased to sponsor the essay as "a vigorous and penetrating analysis of the situation in the south" or something like that.

Since I have this opportunity, let me share a thought I had for Liberation that I broached at the Peacemakers. There's too much emphasis on protesting the injustice and not enough toward the remedy of the situation. The sit-ins are a good case in point. It seems to me that pacificist white folk in general have been taking an evasive tack, namely showing sympathy or going along as fellows. Is that *our* whole business? We are also whites and must confront the causes in the whites. Since I think they are, in an important sense, demented, this means behaving toward them as we do with crazy friends or as one might behave in an epidemic (a matter for the Public Health Service). Put it this way. The negroes have the problem that they have been injured and insulted; therefore it is their immediate job to affirm themselves. Sitting with them expresses the simple meaning that *"People* have been insulted, we have been insulted, and won't put up with it." Very good—but this mainly advantages, I think, the white sitters. The southerners do *not* take them as just people, but as "nigger lovers," and this is significant. To *solve the problem* requires more than the negro victory, it requires confronting the whites. *Our* leaflet should be not "Jim Crow must go" but an application of the standard theory of prejudice: "The reason you've got to feel better than somebody is that you're so browbeaten by your boss, etc.; the reason you folks suffer from fantasies about black penises is that you don't accept your own desires, etc. etc." Naturally this would have to be designed by competent physicians. Personally, I would be afraid to hand out that leaflet, I've been socked in the jaw too often.

In general, less on protest and methods—more on causes and remedies.

Affectionately,

●

[*I tried rather hard to get this letter printed; in vain. It was written in response to the excitement and immense publicity about the sending of troops to cover the entrance of James Meredith into the University of Mississippi.*

In that episode, it seemed to me, the moral issue was entirely lost, and there was mainly satisfaction in the use of force and the imposing of will. Kennedy did not use his moral auhority; he did not go to Oxford, take Meredith by the hand, and into the school. If he had then been hit by a bottle—he might well have—there would have been a great change in the southern liberals. The sane would have ceased cowering. But this matter was handled like all others in our Cold War world.]

October 9, 1962

Editor, *New York Post*

Dear Sir:

Please allow me to say something that needs saying about the liberal attitude, and the coverage of the liberal press, on racial integration and negro civil rights. These are matters of social justice and the unity of mankind. Period. Social justice is worth dying for; the unity of mankind is a basic article of our faith. Period.

But as these matters are at present being treated they seem to me to be used as a smokescreen for, rather than a part of, the crucial issues of our times: peace and the quality of life under modern conditions in this country and increasingly in the world. Civil rights for this disenfranchised group will make as little difference to our degenerating future as civil rights for women have done. I fear that the liberals press so hard in this area because it is a safe kind of revolution.

Sincerely,

•

[On a ceremonial article on Thomas Jefferson, which offended me—I am a Jeffersonian—by emphasizing just that part of him which is convenient to exculpate our totally non-Jeffersonian society. The Times found no room for it.]

April 9, 1962

Editor, *New York Times Sunday Magazine*

Dear Sir,

In his essay on Thomas Jefferson (April 8), I do not think that Professor Padover does justice to Jefferson's continual emphasis on decentralizing power (including a considerable tolerance for local uprisings like Shays' rebellion). For Jefferson, the most essential political principle was the enlightenment of the electorate. The purpose of freedom and democracy was to educate better men, who could then also democratically rule. And he held that it is only by fairly direct initiative in community affairs that people can learn.

Let me give an instance. In designing his epitaph, Jefferson singled out the Declaration of Independence, the Virginia Statute of religious freedom, and the founding of the University of Virginia as the most important acts of his life; yet he said, "Were it necessary to give up either primary education or the University, I should abandon the last, because it is safer to have a whole people respectably enlightened than a few in a high state of science and the many in ignorance." And his plan for these most important primaries was to have them controlled by the smallest possible political unit, the hundreds or militia-companies.

At present we do not have in this country anything that Jefferson would recognize as a free people or the rule of a free people. The excessive centralization and standardization that have developed have made direct democratic control impossible. This has inevitably debased the electorate. We have gone against Jefferson's advice. But even worse, he would have been appalled at the systematic public-relations propagandizing of the public by the mass media, the political parties, the corporations, and even the universities. Would not Professor Padover have done more honor to Jefferson by pointing out these home truths, instead of using his name as a ceremonial ornament for the very kind of society he abhorred?

Yours,

•

[*In* Liberation, *Nov. 1958.*]

October 22, 1958

Editors of *Liberation*

Sirs:

I dislike to disagree sharply with A. J. Muste, of whom I have an affectionate idea, though I do not know him personally. But his critique of "intentional community" in your September issue misses the middle of the target in a most disheartening way.

Speaking of Brookwood, he says, "A sense of spiritual comradeship existed which is felt to this day (more than thirty years later) by dozens of the old graduates." There you have it! Doesn't this strike him as intensely significant? It is not unusual, it is the kind of under-the-skin intimacy that develops among any group that lives and eats together day by day, whether soldiers, or collegians at school, or kids at a summer-camp; yet if in this intimacy there is also taken for granted an excellent common purpose and a shared ethics that makes for living well, what further justification is required? We have a good in itself.

Let me simply repeat Coleridge's complaint against the economist who had said that certain self-sufficient rural villages were valueless because they did not add to the national trade—"What!" cried Coleridge, "is not the existence of 500 Christian souls of value?"

Instead of seeing it this way, Muste says, "If we profess to conceive of mankind as a family which should live as a family, then our only valid objective is the transformation of society, not the building of a shelter for saints or a secular elite within a corrupt social order, which is in effect assumed to be beyond redemption." This is needlessly sarcastic. For cannot we conceive that the persons of the community may regard themselves not as saintly or elite in any way, but simply as making a wiser choice how to get the most richness out of daily life, whether happiness or grief, by being face to face rather than scurrying about looking for brief human contacts in relations that are pretty abstract? The others are not "beyond redemption" but simply unavailable to a close enough acquaintance to know what really to do for them, or what really *you* can do for them. You cannot love everybody, but only your neighbor. You can know *him* only vaguely. I am afraid that on Muste's principle of loving "all the children of God," we come to loving nobody at all, with a good deal of fanatical benevolence expended on secondary issues like wages-and-hours rather than bread and vocation. Then, when Muste says "one other consideration which has kept me . . . from community life is that the impulse which draws a good many in that direction is an ascetic one which I do not share." I wonder whether just the contrary is not the case: that the impulse toward community is a profoundly pleasurable one, on the level of animal touch and so-called infantile security, whereas the drive toward universal welfare and so-called realism is an ascetic resignation of the struggle to be here-now happy.

What is the relation of the community and the rest of society? Muste attacks "the justification of an intentional community as . . . a model of how society should, and eventually might, be organized." But such a justification, I submit, would occur only to an admiring outsider, as we praise the *kvutza* for inventing the right upbringing of children and say we can learn from that in America. But in the community itself, they are solving a problem of living together; and *it is just because they can draw on their face-to-face contact, and therefore are able to argue out their morals as they go along, that they are able to change them and invent something new.* Community is not a model according to an a priori scheme, but a physical cause drawing on powerful social energy.

Conversely, a community is impinged on by the outside, economically and, more importantly, culturally: the cultural attractions of the big world make the community seem insipid and limited, especially to its growing young who have not tasted the dregs. This impingement is not by choice or plan, it is just a fact, and it is a fortunate fact. For once a community has established itself, it is this "outside" that provides the real problems that the group must cope with. It must raise its standard of life to compete (though not necessarily its standard of living); it must find a deeper meaning in itself, and in service to the "outside," to make it worthwhile to continue. Just think of it: if a free community, uncoerced by force or superstitious fear and repression, can in fact maintain itself as worthwhile against the general culture, do you think it will not have unearthed treasures, that it will not have invented a style?

Yours,

[*The theme of face-to-face community which I here develop is of course characteristic of my writing. May I point out, to avoid misundersanding, that I am by no means necessarily thinking of rural communities, though such life is good and charming. A city of 7 millions like New York could be wisely administered, in important respects, like 3500 neighborhoods of 2000. And some of the most important functional advantages of community can be attained by families in a tenement house*

*if they keep their doors open to one another and yet learn to
preserve one another's frequent need not to be disturbed. Also
a gang-system of employment, a "collective contract," as in large
industrial plants in Coventry, that allows for major parts of
the work process to be decided by conversation among the
workers, is feasible in much of our economy and would immensely humanize our lives.]*

•

[*I was asked to give a talk in Professor William Kolb's semi-
nar on the sociology of city-planning, at Carleton College. The
following is the edited tape of the talk and of the subsequent
discussion, as printed in the* Carleton Miscellany, Summer
*1962. The more interesting part is, certainly, the discussion,
for the students were bright and pugnacious.*]

All areas of planning must be treated as a unity. It can't
be helped. If you're going to do any good physical or social planning, you'll find the areas *will* be unified because
the human animals are unified. I'm a pretty ignorant man.
I have, except perhaps as a literary critic, no special knowledge. I am, though, a little bit of a philosopher. And what
I see is just the fact that things hang together and you
can't be very wise unless you are willing to let them hang
together.

I'll give you an instance of unwisdom in recent planning literature, in Jane Jacobs' new book *The Death and
Life of Great American Cities*. In that book an astounding amount of space is devoted to the fact that the streets
are not safe, and to what must be done to make them safe.
I'd been at conventions with Jane and had heard her on
this subject, and I assumed that she was an old maid. But
that isn't true; she's married and has two children. Now
about a third of her book is devoted to physical arrangements to make streets safe, for example adequate lighting,

but her most serious suggestion is that things must be arranged so that everybody on the street is always under some sort of social surveillance. So she's against parks and housing projects with back alleys, etc. I myself would find being under social surveillance quite unlivable, and without alleys and basements how will kids, who can't afford hotels, ever have sex? But those are the disadvantages; the question is are there advantages? If she imagines that the lack of safety in New York and Chicago can be cured by some kind of physical planning for social surveillance, she's quite mistaken.

Recently James Conant, who has been investigating the school system of America, came out with a new book, *Slums and Suburbs,* in which he speaks of the social dynamite in our big cities, stored up by a combination of unemployment, especially of negroes, unrealistic school programs, discrimination by employers and labor unions. He suggests various remedies, in the schools and in serving the drop-outs. Now this kind of approach, if it were seriously implemented, which it won't be, *might* do something about safety on the city streets. But arranging the buildings and the entrances for continual social surveillance is not going to do anything for safety. The fact that people are watching does not prevent crime, it merely inhibits freedom. Under dynamite circumstances, a white man can walk down a street or into a hall, or a colored man can walk down a street in Birmingham, and under perfect social surveillance get himself mugged, robbed, or beat up. And all the surveyors will sit back and couldn't care less. No amount of physical planning is going to help that. You have to look at the problem as a problem of human motives.

You can hope for too much from physical planning. What physical planning can do is to facilitate, to actualize, to perfect underlying social motives that are valuable.

If there is a valuable friendliness among people, then it's possible by a good campus to make a better school. But if there's no real community of faculty and students, and no real interest in real studies, you will not create a school spirit by planning a campus. I think this isn't said enough, though it seems to be such a simple thing. Planning is done in isolation from what's being planned for, and from the social, economic, and political conditions that prevail. In such a case the ideal plan becomes a sort of trap, a trap even worse than no plan.

At present in New York City, in Boston, even Cleveland, certainly Chicago, the big problem for social planning is the fact of segregation, the dis-integrating of neighborhoods. It's happening this way: There's tremendous migration from the south to a certain number of northern cities, especially in the east. The migrants are for the most part young people, as migrants almost always are. These young people have children. That's the nature of young people. At the same time that they are coming to the city, there's an emigration of young, middle-class white people to the suburbs. These too are the ones who have the children. The result is that although the population of Manhattan is not quite 50% colored, a much greater proportion of the children are colored. So the schools are 70%, 90%, 100% segregated. For some reason the others, the young whites, have fled to the suburbs. It's not precise what they are fleeing *from*, but they are the cause of the *de facto* segregation. Forty years ago, when I was a boy in New York, we had integrated schools, and now we don't, and it's the same in other large cities in the north. The conditions in the colored areas are bad and both confirm and breed prejudice in the inhabitants of those areas just as the whites are prejudiced. Then all the physical planning in the world will not make the streets safe. Further, ill-considered bureaucratic efforts to change these condi-

tions may make them worse. Consider housing, for example. In New York City public housing, if your income
rises above a certain figure, you have to move out. There
couldn't be a more stupid notion. The people in the
neighborhood who apparently can make a go of it even in
this society, and might help others to, are forced out. It
takes real bureaucrats to think of this: they have to satisfy
certain administrative criteria, so the people housed have
to be poor and take a means test.

Obviously if you mean to do any planning to undo segregation, and dangerous streets, you must try to build in
mixtures. The public housing must be built for three
classes, four classes.

There's another problem in our housing projects that
you out here wouldn't know about. There are *moral* criteria for living in public housing. If a woman has too
many men, she is judged immoral and out she goes. Now
it is simply a fact that the *mores* of many urban poor are
not middle-class. They are not, in many cases, going to
live in little families of man, wife, and children. Not un-
commonly a woman will have had several children by several different men. Or the woman might go out and work
—there is no breadwinning man—and the children are
then called in the school jargon "latchkey children," they
return after school and let themselves in with their keys.
Now these are simply facts. But the housing is planned in
terms of middle-class conventions for people who do not
have these conventions. It isn't a matter of morals at all;
middle-class morals are not the only morals.

Therefore I'm beginning to recommend as a feature of
public housing the experiment of a dormitory for the teenagers, beginning, say, at age 11. The teenagers will live in
the dormitory as in a youth house in primitive societies.
At the same time, their parents live in the same housing.
The kids have some place to go for solace and advice, and

dinner. They might eat breakfast in the dormitory, lunch at school, and dinner with mama. Then, if mama has a new gentleman home, less hatred might be generated. If these are the facts of life, planning must be adapted to the facts and yet try to bring out something new. In my opinion, this dormitory arrangement would be preferable for the middle class too. Indeed, I wouldn't advise it for anybody unless I thought it would be good for me and my children.

Let's move on. I have started with the smaller units of planning, housing. Let us move to neighborhoods. As you know, most of the advanced and sociologically minded city-planners of the last generation have latched on to neighborhood planning as the right thing. There has been a resurgence of interest in community, the face-to-face group, as the basis for diminishing the anomie and loneliness of mass society—and one of the crimes of big slum-clearance and big public housing has been the disruption of neighborhood ties. But this attitude too can become mechanical. It is felt that the meeting together of people in shopping-centers, for example, will take away the blight of the super-metropolis and megalopolis.

But to make neighborhood planning work, the physical planning is only trivially important compared to the really important thing: neighborhood function. And in order to make any community-function work as community, you must give the community authority, power to make decisions. The only way you will ever get any neighborhood planning that amounts to anything is to dare to decentralize the administration and allow local initiative. Of course you can't *give* initiative; but you can give people the right to exercise initiative and make crucial decisions. (It is said that one person in ten is a "leader." That is enough, if the others have face-to-face access to him.)

Consider it this way: it is not the bigness of cities that

does the damage of anomie; for in principle, a population of 6,000,000 can be regarded as 2000 neighborhoods of 3000, with a local town-hall, for health, education, sanitation, police, etc. Naturally many functions require centralization, e.g. transit; but many functions can be efficiently decentralized to the neighborhoods.

Let me develop one, the school system. In New York City we are supposed to have a pretty good system. It is dreadful. But however bad it is academically, administratively it is absurd. I don't know how many of our scandals come out this way, but I'll mention one or two of the more hilarious. At one school there was a great squawk about the building, and the Superintendent came out. There was a hole in the auditorium ceiling, so the room couldn't be used. "Why hasn't this been repaired?" The Principal: "Are you kidding? I've been trying for four years to get somebody down here. In fact, somebody did come two years ago and the roof was fixed, and six months later it fell in again." They looked up the bill. The cost was in the hundreds of thousands of dollars! This is the centralized administration that is supposed to be efficient.

Have you heard of the rat school? The principal is a friend of mine, Elliott Shapiro. He's a saintly type and picked that school because it was one of the worst. Among other things, lots of rats. So he squawked and finally the Mayor appeared. Sure enough, he walked into the building and out jumped a rat right at the Mayor, and there was a picture of it in the *Times!* "This must be attended to immediately!" Top priority. This was in March. In July came the workmen and left their cans of paint. They left their cement to repair the courtyard. But all summer no work was done. School began the second week in September. The third week came the workmen, with a pneumatic drill in the courtyard. You couldn't hold classes because you couldn't hear. The paint dripped on your head, the fumes were sickening. So Elliott, who is very bold, called off classes, and told the children to go home and tell their mothers that school was off because the city hadn't repaired the school in time, and he would not keep children in a dangerous school. The mothers then organized a strike. The city objected to the strike, but finally it got so bad that the city—an election was coming up— had to give in. Children were bussed to other schools; workmen were paid for overtime. Fine. But back in March, two Marches ago, three Marches ago, Elliott could have picked up a phone, called an exterminator in the neighborhood, and said, "Get rid of these damned rats and bill the city." But if he'd done that, he would have landed in the penitentiary, for spending the public money. You have to go through Livingston Street, that's the Board of Education, and when Livingston Street has agreed to get rid of rats, you proceed to the Board of Estimate. Thing like that takes time.

Conceive of the advantages and the dangers of the opposite: the tax money going to the PTA, for instance, to make the kind of school they want to make, with the central Board of Education preserving, let us say, minimum standards and seeing to it that every neighborhood gets a reasonable share of money, so the rich neighborhoods don't hog it all. Also, some services are better centralized: research, licensing (perhaps), medical services, some social and special services for the handicapped, etc. The central Board could carry on all these things without dictating local school policy. The purpose of the central system is to serve the localities, and not the reverse.

It seems to me that this is perfectly feasible. If it were established in the New York system tomorrow, of course, there would be chaos, but even that mightn't be so bad. Some schools would be perfectly terrible, some would be pure John Birch. On the other hand, some would be excellent. (A surprising number of intelligent people might join a PTA if it had any power.) At present there are no excellent schools in our public system. None. You can't have a good school if you can't experiment more freely than is allowed. Given a completely decentralized system, there might be schools worse than our worst. I doubt it but it's possible; all the children might die of cholera. But then people would be making their own mistakes and they'd have to learn real fast! The Board might well advise them and say, "What you're doing won't work. The kids will never get into high school or college." The members of the PTA might get smarter.

In fact, this is how the settlement houses are run. Neighborhood gang work and other kinds of social work are neighborhood projects invented by the project leaders in the settlement houses. They call on the city when they want help. (They don't always get it, but that's the theory anyway.) So far as we have community spirit in our New York neighborhoods, these settlement houses have been a great factor. Clearly localized schools would be an even greater factor.

Even more important, perhaps, are housing and urban renewal. They too could be localized. A reasonable method would be to invite people from a university to make alternative sets of plans for a neighborhood. Perhaps by competition, with a board of architects, etc., to rule out the plans that are just impossible. Perhaps six workable plans will remain. Then you educate people by inviting them to the school. You have a party or bazaar; you explain the plans, and point up the features of this one and that one. You carry on communication for six months, a year. Perhaps the plans become a local political issue. Finally, a vote—whatever they choose they get. No faking. Usually they won't choose the best. How could they possibly? But they'll choose something that will almost surely be better, more fitting their local needs, than what some bureaucrat in the City Planning Commission of New York City will give them. By giving the neighborhoods the power to decide, I think you will eventually get real neighborhoods, and you might even get good plans.

And let me now make a big jump, to the final topic I'd like to discuss. In my opinion, one of the chief things we have to do in order to get better *urban* planning is to reverse somewhat the trend from country to city. Consider. The cities have always been the place where high culture has grown and flourished. For obvious reasons. People mix, crafts and groups mix; there's trade, and people come from far places to trade. The people of the city hear other languages, customs, philosophies, and sciences. This sharpens intelligence. But I don't think it's sufficiently remembered that these exciting cities have always had a definite limit and a pretty close relationship with a countryside. It's one thing to live in a city when you have country cousins whom you visit and they visit you. It's another thing to live in a 600 miles conurbation when you can go and go and go and never get out of the suburbs that have the same city-culture in a more boring form. The city must have a stopping point. Then you might have an entity and begin to improve its center. Think of the money we've spent in New York on escape highways to Long Island, Westchester, Westport in Connecticut, etc. Billions of dollars. And think if we spent the greater part of that money on improving the center, saying, "Here, this is the limit of the city. Around here we'll have some good thick forests for a little way. And after the forest, farms, with cows."

The problem then is how to get people to live on the farms with the cows. Just the reverse is happening. Everybody goes away from the farms that have the cows into the city. The reason is, I think, pretty simple. Besides the fact that there's not enough cash, the farm in some ways is dull. Now the modern city is even duller, but the farmboy doesn't know that. It's exciting when he first arrives. It's importantly a question of morals, of impossible morals in the farm community. The kind of moral repression that is possible when, as was the case, temptations remained in the unconscious and were never thought of, is impossible when the contents have been thought of. For moral repression then becomes plain inhibition, and nobody can lead an inhibited life. You can't take people with certain repressive moral customs and surround them with an urban culture in which quite different things are acceptable and advertised—the TV, the movies, and all the rest of it—and expect that those people are going to be content and happy as they were. They are continually stimulated, the old repression breaks down, and then the country life becomes unacceptable and the young go to the city. Of course they do.

They make a mistake, because the place they go to may be freer in some respects, but it doesn't have many other desirable qualities. And the quality of city life is made dull when it is no longer related to the country. We must then find some way to build new patterns of life in the country and the small town and so diminish the urban migration.

Take your Northfield, for example. If new industries were brought in, so there'd be more cash, especially if they were interesting industries, then you'd have industry, a farming community, and the two colleges. That could be a very exciting community if in fact everybody shared in all three activities. If every family had one boy or girl in the college, and one in the factory, and one on the farm, and yet they all lived together, as you can in a place of this size, you would begin to get a very interesting life with cross fertilization of ideas, a life which, on the whole, would be better than in an urban spread. That kind of pattern might help to stop the urban migration, and perhaps partly reverse it. I've talked enough.

QUESTION: You have been called a utopian thinker on the ground that the things you propose cannot conceivably be achieved. How do you move in the direction of getting these things done?

ANSWER: If any of these things are to be accomplished they must be accomplished by pressure. The important thing is to try to make the unit of pressure the small local unit, the renewal of which is one of the things you're trying to accomplish. In trying to achieve decentralization in the city, for example, it is the settlement house, the school, the neighborhood that should be exercising the pressure, not the election district, the aim being that the neighborhood finally *becomes* the election district.

Q. If the desire for power corrupts, as well as power, and if the neighborhood settlement house had charge of its own budget, and the budget was public money, wouldn't your neighbors like to climb from their place in the hierarchy to the place which would inevitably be there, the tax collector's office and the disbursement office at the top?

A. No, no, I don't think so. I don't think so because I think the corruptibility of mankind is caused by frustration. People don't want power as such. What they want is activity. They want to actualize potentialities, and insofar as they want power they want it in order to make decisions, in order to act. Now in a situation where more and more rights to make decisions are taken away from people, there gets to be more and more need to identify with big decision makers. But in a family, for instance, where decision making remains, a pretty much allright family let's say, isn't there pretty much of a continual town meeting going on?

Q. Not if mama controls the purse strings, as mama does pretty often.

A. Now wait a minute. Papa brings home the money and both mama and the kids have pressures whereby they get the money from him. But what are they? My kids have pretty good pressures. Some of their pressures largely consist in the fact that the activity their money is going for seems so worthwhile, that I want them to have it. And once that is established, in fact there *are* no unreasonable demands ever made. After a while if one of them would say to me I want five bucks, I wouldn't even ask what he wanted it for, because I know it would be used well. It always is. Because there hasn't been at the beginning a denial of his activity. And I don't think that's extraordinary. Do you?

Q. It seems to me there's a valid point that's been lost somewhere here. A great part of the time, perhaps due to the fact that frustration is inevitable, there are power struggles. Let's acknowledge this first, and then your idea of neighborhoods can be talked about in terms of more available power.

A. That's right.

Q. Somebody almost inevitably is going to be holding that power, some one person or small group.

A. I don't see why that follows. What was the idea of our federal system to begin with?

Q. What happened, though?

A. Well, yes, but, did it have to happen? You're saying it had to happen.

Q. Just a pure empirical argument: it does happen.

A. But that isn't altogether true. We tend to be very blind to those cases where it hasn't been true. Let's take the history of science. Up to the last thirty years, you'll find that science has been run in an international and completely decentralized way. Perfectly. There've been scientific academies, there've been universities that cooperated. They've advanced science by leaps and bounds; each little group has been in charge of its funds. And there hasn't been much of an attempt by anybody to dominate from above.

Q. I'm going to pick on this one, because I don't think you have a valid example, simply because there isn't much conflict of basic personal importance.

A. Oh, the devil that's so!

Q. Well, maybe there wasn't any need for this degree of organization before.

A. Scientific work has been extremely organized. I never said it wasn't organized. In every country there were academies of science, conventions, publications. The organization was immense, but there was no power struggle in the sense of some group struggling for centralized domination.

Q. There wasn't any need for a power struggle.

A. There never is a need for a power struggle. This is a neurosis.

Q. But today big organizations are giving out the money, and if you want any part in research in science you have to have money, and you have to get it from the people who control it.

A. That's right. In other words, what's happened is that we are interfering with this great history of science with goals that are not the ideals of science. But centralization does not have to happen. It's a style exactly the way baroque was a style. In fact it is a baroque style, as Lewis Mumford points out. That's just what baroque planning is: in the middle is the big palace and all the rays come from the center.

Q. You think though that this is not necessary either in science or in the planning of the neighborhood, that we could choose to do otherwise.

A. Choose is too strong a word because choose gives the idea that you can get out of your skin. I think that we

could edge in directions where it would become less necessary to do it this way. Let's put it that way. By creating
other kinds of small institutions, we can take the venom
out of the centralized institution. You have to fight against
it with ideas of alternative activities. You can't fight against
it with words, thought, a beatnik withdrawal. A beatnik
withdrawal, however, is not a bad first step. To stop is
often a very good step. Just to stop, in the beatnik way.
You just won't do it. Then maybe you will think of something else to do.

Q. What kind of children would come out of the dormitory situation you propose?

A. What I was proposing was the family structure of the
kibbutz, and the psychological theory behind it is Freud-
ian. The trouble that leads to the Oedipus complex is the
problem of the good and bad mother. The aim of the kibbutz it to make the mother only the good mother; that is,
she teaches you nothing. She doesn't teach you table manners, you learn table manners from society. But when society gets too rough then you can run home crying and
mama comforts you.

Q. I've heard some conflicting things about the effects
that the kibbutz has had on children.

A. That's why I said to begin at age eleven. It seems beyond doubt that if a child is brought up, especially from
the age of about six months to two years, without personal
attention, he develops a cold personality which may eventually become a psychopathic personality. In Israel it was
not implicit in the notion that the child should not get
individual attention; they placed the child in the kibbutz
too early because they needed the woman's work in the
fields.

Q. I wonder when you talk about putting the children
in a dormitory like that. I would not want to give my children up to someone else.

A. You're living in a dream world, dear. Wait till you have children. You'll find that your children get their standards from the street and not from you.

Q. Well, if they are still living at home and I have some influence on their lives, I might be able at least to modify the standards of the street. But if they are off somewhere else, I can't control them at all.

A. Yes, that's true. But even then if the standards you have at home are really more worthwhile and, what is more important, interesting, the child will get something from them even though he lives in the dormitory. But if we take the average situation, I think that almost any street situation is better than most family situations with regard to standards, culture, or love. Moreover, there is no such thing as absolute power over a child anyway.

Q. I'm not talking about absolute power. I just want to maintain an influence over my children by having them live at home.

A. And I'm saying that in urban slum conditions, by and large, I would rather make the influence a little less.

Q. But you said that you would not recommend anything that you would not do for your own children.

A. That's right.

Q. And I would not want to do it to my children. It would be all right if people agreed to it, but I want mine at home.

A. That's right. That's right. That's why I certainly would recommend any such policy on a voluntary basis.

Q. You mentioned something about the importance of interest. Why does it have this importance?

A. I'll tell you why. There are some things that have to be done against people's wills, but we do them at peril. For instance, if a child drifts out into the traffic, you get him by the neck and swat the tar out of him so that he learns his lesson. But every time that's done or a child is made to do something which isn't interesting to him, he is going to do it with less grace and talent; that is, less of himself initiated from inside is going to be involved in it. So insofar as we're interested in the perfection of everybody's life, we must try as much as we can to have a basis of spontaneous interest for anything that is done. The reason is that it will be done better, more accurately, with more grace, more intelligence, and more force.

Q. Would there be adult supervision in these dormitories?

A. If I were running them there would not be. There would be rules, for there is a necessity for structure. The kids would not be left completely to their own devices, for I would combine the dormitory system with a form of urban renewal which would attempt to give the kids the kinds of jobs which adolescents can do, such as renovation. The kids would not be neglected by adults, for if one comes over to a man working and watches, the man will talk to him. And they will be paid for working in the urban renewal program. Isn't this what happens in a primitive culture: Youth House and community work?

Q. You mentioned that with local planning there might be tremendous messes. What would happen? People might think that the planning was a terrible idea and public opinion might become so strong that the planning could not be carried through.

A. That's right. That's exactly what happened to progressive education when they began to try it. So that instead of giving it a real try, things stopped at the level of minor messes and then panic.

Q. Well what would you suggest doing about this?

A. I would suggest more courage.

Q. If power is given to the small group, who is going to lead its members?

A. The people who are wiser, compassionate.

Q. How are they going to establish themselves in this group?

A. Well, now look. Let's pretend for a moment that since I'm sitting here at the head of the table, I'm wiser. How have I established myself? It's not the physical plan of the room. There is no other answer, except that I care. I care enough to think about it; I care enough to write an article; I care enough to talk about it to other people who know something about it.

Q. Is there anything beside courage that might serve to overcome panic?

A. Well perhaps motivational research might serve the same function at this level, that psychotherapy does at the individual level; that is you use sociological and psychological techniques not in order to put something into the person, but in order to get rid of those things which prevent him from being himself. In psychotherapy we call this unblocking. Thus we might use motivational research to get the people out of the idea that the planning can't be done. That would be quite sufficient. Then I would rather let nature take its course, so that the community is natural. I really deeply think so.

Q. Somewhere you have described yourself as an anarchist. What do you mean by that?

A. I'm for diminishing the exercise of coercive authority as much as possible. I don't think there's any anarchist thought at present which is interested in a total revolution of society or has any picture of a total society. The aim in general is to turn involuntary organizations into voluntary organizations, to turn as much as possible the pre-organized into the spontaneously organized. To remove as far as possible the principle of fear as a strong force in human relations so that other feelings will emerge, such as anger, love, excitement, interest.

Q. I don't understand what you would do, if, for instance, on a small community level the majority of the members decide to do this or that, and an individual or a few individuals are outvoted.

A. In principle in a good society things would not be put to a vote. If there was disagreement nothing would be done. The matter would not be tabled forever, because people would keep attempting to understand the others' point of view, for the motives of all would be trusted. But frequently things can be decided fairly easily. Suppose you go out with a few friends and one says let's go to this movie and another says let's go to a different movie. How is it decided?

Q. You vote.

A. Oh, you do not. What happens is that somebody really cares and really wants to go to a particular movie, and the others don't really care that much and say O.K. Isn't that what would happen in a society where people trust one another?

Q. But people don't always have the same set of principles.

A. That's right. And that's another reason for decentralism. When you have a nice decentralized system, those who disagree with the way one neighborhood is run can pack up and find another one more to their liking.

Q. It's pretty obvious that a lot of people want, or think they want, green space, The suburban way of getting green space has produced some fairly undesirable side effects such as sprawl, transportation problems, etc. How can we provide for this desire for green space, given considerably greater density than presently exists in the suburb?

A. Is it really the case that people want the green space? Isn't it possible that when they say they want green space, they're trying to say something but they're confused as to what it is they want; that the green space is a sentimental rationalization for some real need?

Q. If people are merely rationalizing when they say that they need space and green lawns, and they scream about slow bus service and about slums, then all these things and the reaction to them may be a result of the quality of life that we live in America.

A. Doesn't it seem obvious that a large part of the flight to the suburb is an effort to find a place where you have some say in your life?

Q. To get back to the criticism of your work as utopian, there are those who say that people spend a lot of time talking about impossible ideals, the utopias if you will, and that this keeps them from getting down to the things which actually might be accomplished.

A. I think that there is a false estimate of the general public involved here. The basis of this sort of criticism is the conception that the average man does not have profound ideals, that he doesn't have high hopes and castles in the air. In fact, the more simple people are, the more they tend to go in for future thinking. But because there is so much potential conflict in such ideas, the people who want to get elected soft-pedal them. It is a matter of how people really are, and therefore of what is *really* feasible.

Q. What is feasible though is partly dependent on the present organization of society.

A. I would suggest ameliorating the present organization. This can be done by people who withdraw from the larger society to carry on experimentation in new patterns, or it can be done by centralized planning for decentralization.

Q. But to get that central plan you'd have to have a fight in the center of power politics.

A. That's right, that's why I bother to write books. But

this notion that the central plan would have to support further centralization is a myth which has been foisted by certain big industrialists on you. It is a germ which they put into your mind, a disease. There has been nothing like it in the history of mankind.

Q. What about the farm problem, the farm problem that is centrally managed from Washington? That wasn't foisted on anybody by industrialists. It was foisted on our country by simple laws of economic growth.

A. No, I don't believe that, I don't believe it. If you go back you'll see that there was every encouragement for not doing diversified farming, but for doing cash crop farming. This was altogether unnecessary. The farmer fell into a trap.

Q. We all recognize then that the problems of the city are not only the problems of the city but also of the suburb.

A. I think suburbs ought to be wiped out. They are a bad idea. Get rid of them.

Q. What happens if the people who live in the suburbs are delegated decentralized power and choose to live in the suburbs?

A. Well, now look. If all the brass and the intellectual planners begin to set their minds against the suburban fringe, we have to assume that this will create a new cultural tone. It must be so.

Q. This will be education and not manipulation?

A. I think so.

Q. One of the troubles is just plain sheer numbers of people. When we first moved out of the city we weren't moving to the suburbs but rather to the country. But the country later became the suburbs.

A. What do you mean, sheer numbers of people? You can't mean actual population growth? I don't see crowds when I look out the window here. This crowding in the suburbs isn't because of an increase of population. It is caused by redistribution. And you can set up counterforces in the suburb to go in the other direction. Tax policy, road policy, FHA policy. Or take Cape Cod National Park. It is going to say "no further" and it is also saying "we will buy up the land of people who move out."

Q. But then the city will expand and overtake the suburb.

A. Yes, but it is also possible to set up forces in the direction of keeping people from going to the suburb or the city, to keep them in the small town and the farm.

Q. Some day there just won't be room to stay on the farm.

A. That's a long time from now, and I don't believe it —I mean, I'm not convinced.

Q. How long is a long time?

A. That depends on what population figures you study. I frankly think this business of the population explosion is a somewhat bourgeois notion, and it is also something of a red herring which is thrown in the way of settling immediate problems. Why suddenly bring this neo-Malthusianism into the picture? They said the same thing exactly in the time of Malthus.

5

FAILURE OF INTELLECT

●

Editor, *The New York Times*

Dear Sir,

   May I congratulate the writer of the leading editorials of
the *Times* on his finally achieving to perfection the diplo-
matic style of M. de Norpois in Proust? It is a striking
proof that America has become mature and the greatest.
I doubt that any other world capital than New York could
now carry off this manner. The leader of Sunday, May 6
was especially fine. From the very first sentence, "Armed
with a good cause and the shield of defensive military
might made more potent by our nuclear tests, President
Kennedy is now engaged in a new effort to find some sort
of accommodation with Soviet Russia to avert an atomic
Armageddon," we have the authentic mastery: celebrating
whatever the case happens to be, concluding from it nothing in particular, being modestly indefinite about any next

action, and being professionally traditional in the termi-
nology. The following from the middle is even more
beautiful: "Since the status quo cannot be changed except
by force, which is unacceptable in the atomic age, a modus
vivendi based on it is the only practical solution for the
moment." But, of course, the best is at the end: "Secretary
Rusk is certainly not too optimistic. But he, like most
Western statesmen, is confident that we are 'moving with
the winning currents of history,' etc." Who today could
match this?

May I suggest, however, that there is too much repro-
duction in your pages of Mr. Kennedy's face? Sometimes
half a dozen times in a single issue. This is vulgar—a "cult
of personality," as they used to say of Stalin.

Yours etc.,

[*Not printed.*]

•

[*Some British and American astronomers have been sending
code-signals into distant space on the theory that among the
millions of habitable planets there must be many more technically advanced than we, who might catch our signals and
respond. These astronomers often display a, to me, comical
lack of imagination that the culture of others might have
developed in a way unthinkably different from ours.*

*But inevitably there has sprung up a rival school that warns
against letting these outsiders know we exist, because they will
surely come down and eat us up. Mr. Ubell did not acknowledge the following letter.*]

April 19, 1962

Science Editor, *New York Herald-Tribune*

Dear Earl Ubell:

In your speculation of April 17 about the dangers of
space communication, you commit a vulgar and very per-

nicious fallacy. If those on Tau Centi would be a million years ahead of us technically, we might hope that they might be at least a little wiser than we are, and have more universal and disinterested aims. If we were like insects to them, they might be like true naturalists toward us, curious, loving, and conserving. Though they might not "empathize," they might certainly understand and sympathize, like Darwin or Fabre. I rather doubt that any beings could be worse for men than men are for themselves.

What is pernicious and unscientific about your thinking is that you assume that the particular mores of warfare and competition that we now suffer are unchanging facts, rather than phenomena of our culture and history. You vulgarly project into space the strategies of our present Cold War. Certainly it is better for scientists to pursue, with naive faith, all knowledge and all avenues of knowledge (including exchanging signals!). Otherwise the human adventure is hardly worth while.

Sincerely,

●

August 30, 1962

Editor, *The Boston Globe*

Dear Sir,

I must protest the remark of Robert Frost, as reported in your issue of August 30th, that a nation must have "power" to "protect the language, to protect the poetry." I think that any competent judgment of English literature in this century would say that a thumping majority of the very greatest figures were Irish, e.g. Yeats, Synge, Joyce, Shaw. Similarly, Rilke and Kafka, who wrote in German, were Czech. As the Jews have long known, it is best to make use of a "world power" language and culture, but not to be hampered by the prejudices, brutality, and foolishness that belong to "power."

Yours,

[*Not printed.*]

●

[*For its Commencement issue of June 9, 1961, the Brandeis University* Justice *sent a questionnaire to "twenty outstanding Americans representing different fields and opinions." The questions were: (1) Do you believe there will be a nuclear war? (2) What do you believe are the possibilities for a rapprochement between the Soviet Union and the United States? (3) Students of modern industrial society have noted the repressive nature of the world in which we live. To what extent do you believe that our culture will become more or less repressive? (4) What future do you see for the arts in competition with mass culture in our society? (5) What do you believe is the most vital issue facing our generation and the world?*]

To the Editor of *The Justice*

Dear Sir,

Except for your last question, you ask for probabilities and predictions. I am neither able nor willing to give them. Predictions may be either prophetic or scientific. Prophetic predictions would be legitimate in these issues since, because of his peculiar relation to the source of power, a prophet can make them come to pass. But a scientific prediction is the logical consequence of an hypothesis and a process of reasoning leading to an experiment that one will make to test the prediction and hypothesis. In such vital issues as you raise, we do not want a test, we want a state of affairs to become and be; it is incumbent on us to make it be. So this practical aim might as well be stated right off, and your question ought to be, "How to prevent nuclear war? How to make mass-communications

good for something? etc." When one is faced with problems, predictions—or sentiments of optimism or pessimism
—are irrelevant luxuries. For one has to cope anyway with
the question, Then what? whose only answer will be to do
something about the vital issues. So better, Now what?

PESSIMISTIC QUESTIONS

Wording the questions as you do (a) *creates* the attitude
that one can be a detached predicter about such issues;
and (b) since one is then not practically engaged, one has
to make one's judgment from a global view of the situation
"as it is," as if it were not obviously wretched. To start
with a wretched situation and make predictions about it,
rather than pitching into it with practical questions about
problems, is the same as detaching oneself from the situation. And this is the same as going to New Zealand, the
furthest available place. That might be a wise choice, but
then it should be affirmed as such and your first question
ought to be about tickets to New Zealand, from where one
can make sporty predictions and calculate the betting odds.

I am therefore in a position to answer your last question, about the most crucial issue facing the world. It is
the propensity of the editors of *The Justice* to believe that
"Nothing really can be done," and therefore to ask questions in a discouraging form. Conversely, it is my propensity to scold them this way, rather than to employ physical
and psychotherapeutic means to shake them out of it. But
you are legion and distant; your home professors will have
to do it.

TWO WORLDS

With regard to the other questions, what would be my
grounds for a prediction? I know face to face, and man-

ageably, a fairly large number of persons. (By "manage-
ably" I do not mean that I can influence them, but that
I can plausibly try.) Now among these, I know and somewhat do actions that can have some effect in diminishing
the chances of war, in humanizing industry, in heighten-
ing honesty and earnestness of speech. Some of them even
—these are my friends—agree with me and cooperate with
me. Thus, by this particular idiosyncratic sampling of the
population, I would make one set of predictions. (And we
do act as if we made these predictions, for we act without
despair, although doggedly.)

On the other hand, if I read the papers, listen to the
radio, and so forth, I seem to be in a world of quite different people. It is not so much that they are making mistakes, easy or hard to correct, but as if they had a different
sensibility from mine. They seem to find tolerable what
to me is dismaying; they can stomach what makes me
vomit; they are entertained by what bores me; they make
prejudiced and censorious judgments about things that to
me are not a big deal. And the people of that world are
probably unreachable by any stratagems that I see in operation that could prevent nuclear war, humanize industry
or increase honest speech. So using them as evidence, I
have to make another set of predictions. That is, on the
one hand I judge from myself and my 200 friends and our
3000 correspondents; on the other, I have to judge from,
apparently, the scores of millions who constitute the world
of *The New York Times,* the Luce publications, and as
far as NBC and CBS. This discrepancy of numbers would
seem to settle the matter.

A COMMON HUMANITY

But of course, like a good Kantian and Jeffersonian,
I do not believe for a moment that there are these two

grades of humanity. There is a common sensibility of mankind. Now I know that my friends and I are human. I therefore assume that the world reflected in the mass press and radio is a fiction, a pathological delusion, and (often demonstrably) a plain lie. Such stolid confidence as I have does not depend on the voices of us happy—and dismayed—few against a consensus of deluded millions; but on the possible unspoken common sense and reachable good feeling in all of us scores of millions of human beings. *Will* this common reason speak? *Will* this benevolence be reached, rebel, and act? Ah, here is the crux where one cannot afford the luxury of predictions because there are practical problems of witnessing, social inventiveness, and psychotherapy.

MORAL AND POLITICAL

Let me say only that I rarely, almost never, meet a person who, with any effort of contact between us, is such a fool or rogue as the public picture of the common American: almost nobody who could believe in either Kennedy or Nixon or their parties, who thinks that the TV is anything but trash, who takes war-talk as anything but psychotic. I meet very many who imagine that the faults of the economic and industrial system are pretty inevitable; but I have found that when real alternatives are sketched out to them, they show lively interest and are as if eager to be convinced. People want to hear *how* centralization and bureaucracy can be diminished, how scientific technology need not involve increasing mass-ignorance, how mass-communications can be domesticated. The kinds of issues that you raise are not sociological and technological; they are not subject to scientific predictions. They are moral and political.

Viewing the world from *your* point of view, however,

I should like to say that your questions are hopelessly un-realistic. Given the operators in power, we are likely to have fascism in this country in two or three years, and *that* will pose (for such Americans as still have some morale and culture) very absorbing problems.

•

October 23, 1960

Editor, *Columbia University Forum*

Dear Sir,

Saul Engelbourg's article in your Fall issue is excellent. The attempt he makes at the end to distinguish the individual's own "utility level" from the "utility level of other people" seems to me to be an ingenious and original stab in the direction of a new kind of calculation that is much needed. May I make a general observation?

It is perhaps unwise to continue to call this kind of discussion, or much of the discussion in Galbraith's *Affluent Society*, by the name of Economics. The case is probably that classical Political Economy is a *completed science,* like Euclidean geometry or the Aristotelian theory of the syllogism. Historically, the problems of political economy have been the allocation of resources in scarcity, the diminishing of scarcity, and the avoidance of fluctuation. In principle these problems are solved; and the sign is that our economists increasingly begin to think of individual values not conveniently subject to statistical handling, and cultural or even moral values not subject to such handling at all. It is a question of a word whether or not such topics should be called "economic," but the danger of calling them "economic" is that the economist-writers, who have a flair for them and could be very valuable to society, have not yet realized that to treat such questions they have to learn new disciplines, psychological, moral, and political, which are as yet foreign to them.

Sincerely,

[*Printed in the Winter issue.*]

•

[*The Council for Correspondence—formerly "Committee for Correspondence" but there proved to be a conflict of name with an organization of the Daughters of the American Revolution!—is a clearing-house for intellectuals with hopefully practical ideas to meet the threat of total nuclear disaster. I have occasionally contributed, but in general have been disappointed at their almost universal tendency to play war games and diplomacy within the framework of the Powers creating the threat and making a solution impossible. The issue of The Council for Correspondence's Newsletter of October, 1962, a post mortem on the recent Cuba crisis, roused me to repeat my usual complaint, this time to David Riesman.*]

December 4, 1962

Dear Dave,

Let me object to your remark in the October issue: "We may be too nihilistic and too cynical, rejecting the nation-state as do Paul Goodman and A. J. Muste. Many people are almost glad when the big powers behave badly, because they reject the big power system as such. . . . This is a self-defeating course (there may be no other), since we have the big powers, etc."

I think it is the *Newsletter's* position that is nihilistic. (None of us is cynical.) If in fact powers act as they do and must, being what they are—and the point of my little essay in *Liberation* was to analyze their nature—the serious attitude toward them must be to try to limit the damage they do by weakening support of them. The only way to make powers tolerable to live with is to squawk and balk till they fear they may lose their control and power— which we, in turn, do *not* want to assume. This is the only language that they *can* understand.

"When they act badly": in our view, they cannot act well, whether with regard to armaments, or the University of Mississippi, or improving TV. They cannot because they are not primarily interested in useful function, but in maintaining and aggrandizing power. Therefore their more or less moderate behavior is entirely unreliable for our uses. It never merits approval; it must be met by various degrees of apprehensiveness and, at present, a persistent effort to diminish power, because it is too damned dangerous.

A repeated theme of the October issue was that the U.S. government has failed to enlighten its electorate, has merely represented its prejudices, etc. Certainly. But when you people persistently blink at the true nature of power —even when you probably agree with us—then you too confuse the electorate. It is quite irresponsible to speak, as you do, of "the grievous limits of the international system," and not keep urging toward the revolutionary alternative. You keep giving "critical support" to Kennedy exactly as the Trotskyists give "critical support" to Kruschev. This is miserable pedagogy. People are thirsting for a real alternative that is *not* admittedly evil. To explore this and develop it is the proper use of intellect. You people muddy up the water and are, it seems to me, a typical *trahison des clercs*.

There is not much hope that enlightenment about the power-system will first spread widely in this country or in the Soviet Union. There is more hope of headway in England, Italy, perhaps Poland. A groundswell in Europe might begin to alter sentiment here. For heaven's sake, do not make them feel that the Americans are incorrigible.

What is brutal is how Africa and Latin America have gotten sucked into the power system, because they cannot conceive of alternatives. And it is clear (e.g. from India) that "neutralism" is not a viable alternative when the going gets rough. In international relations, as in civil liberties, a holding operation does not even hold; only an on-going revolutionary effort to diminish power and extend freedom can maintain even the peace and freedom we have.

To use the usual rhetoric: the opposing generals always have more in common with one another than either has with his own troops. If somebody took a pot-shot at one K., the other would at once send him a telegram of concern, because it's a bad precedent.

Best,

•

[Review for *Sunday Book Review, The New York Times,* November 11, 1962.]

ALL THE WAY DOWN, The Violent Underworld of Street Gangs. By Vincent Riccio and Bill Slocum. (Simon and Schuster)

This is the report of a spell with the Youth Board by an energetic young man of average intelligence and sensibility, but with an athletic body and a strong affection for kids. It ends with his quitting street-work to become a high-school teacher and coach, largely because of disrespect for the bureaucracy of the Board and his judgment that the work does not offer enough advancement and money for his growing family. His present feeling is regretful and despairing. The work was important and exciting, but he accomplished little; the obstacles are overwhelming, and the conditions are deteriorating. He is concerned especially about the increase in drug-addiction, leading to ever longer prison-terms and sudden death from overdose. It is worthwhile to review the book because of Riccio's exemplary ordinariness, in his values and motives and in the journalistic telling of the delicate texture of living (helped by Bill Slocum of the *Daily Mirror*). Riccio seems to be a good joe, unusually outspoken, fairly courageous, and altogether unradical. In the upheaval of our urbanism, the baseness of our economy and politics, and the breakdown of conventional morals, we are in a more revolutionary situation than this kind of values and style can cope with.

Rick's frankness is refreshing. He detests the New York Police who are no doubt a fine body of men but who, in his almost universal experience, are brutes and grafters. He has contempt for Harry Anslinger and the Narcotics squad—"Mr. Anslinger has been leading the war against addiction for over thirty years. Need I say more?" He is impatient with the Youth Board brass for endangering its workers and hurting kids just in order to allay public hysteria. (I do not follow Bill Slocum in the *Mirror,* but I wonder how he copes with the fact that his paper gleefully fans this hysteria. Why doesn't he explode and get fired?)

But Rick's lack of perception of the big enemies of the kids (and himself) is painful. He has an inkling that the disruption of neighborhoods by our ghetto housing is a cause of bad trouble, but there is no anger against Webb and Knapp or Robert Moses; how does he think the buildings get there? In one passage he compares gang rumbles to wars and points out that "only the psychopaths and some of the generals want war," but he taught judo and combat hand-to-hand fighting in the Navy, and we do not read that he led his kids into the Worldwide General

Strike for Peace. There is no discussion of the school-system that has let his kids down. He is realistic in most sexual matters, but silent about the role of his church in giving the kids a bad conscience and taking the innocent joy out of their lives.

But even more disturbing than the book's lack of philosophy is that Riccio shares and reinforces many of the delinquent traits that stunt his kids' growth. He naively boasts of conning the kids—e.g. concerning their boxing prowess—as if they could be cured without being taken seriously as persons. He encourages them to act for reputation rather than the value of the activity itself. He even outdoes them in his contempt for eggheads. He rails at city urchins' fear of the dark and wild animals, but cannot make therapeutic use of the nerve of fright, hostility, and instinct-anxiety that they have thereby exposed. Indeed, often the dramatic tone of his little scenes is of a contest of wills between stubborn siblings. Naturally, then, the kids like Rick, because he is useful and kindly; but they can hardly get out of themselves by means of him, for he is no wiser or more interesting than they are.

Riccio's chief positive proposal in this book is the adoption of the English system of legalizing heroin under medical prescription and treatment. His arguments for this are the standard ones of the social-scientists (though throughout he is disdainful of sociologists and psychologists): to destroy the economic motive of the pushers and to integrate the addiction into a quiet and hopefully curative milieu. I wish he would learn to extrapolate the same attitude to the kids' other hang-ups. The cure for their violent sexuality is to allow them guiltless sex. The cure for their defiance is to teach them their real enemies to fight. The cure for their foolish activism is to provide them a world that has worthwhile tasks.

164 :

●

[Review for *Sunday Book Review, The New York Times,*
June 24, 1962.]

ANOTHER COUNTRY. By James Baldwin. (Dial Press)

The barriers of prejudice between us create new barriers within us—suspicion, self-contempt, the need for
revenge—and these separate us still further. There is a
modern triad of objects of prejudice who internalize the
prejudice: Jews, homosexuals and Negroes.

In *Another Country,* James Baldwin studies the homosexuals and Negroes, often in parallel scenes. His plotting
urges toward the breakdown of the barriers and the recov-
ery of common humanity in love, a love that, in this book,
invariably climaxes in sexual bouts. These are told frankly
and pretty well, the homosexual ones somewhat better
because they are less hectic and abrupt. The divisive barriers, on the other hand, he explores as far as sexual jealousy, and there are scenes of violence.

Unfortunately the persons of *Another Country* exist in
a kind of vacuum: they do not have enough world to grow
in, so love does not lead to community, procreation, pro-
ductive collaboration, character change or even personal
security. The author merely affirms their love to be important. And since there is not enough on-going world to
support the jealous, their jealousy comes merely to sullen-
ness and separation, without insight, liberation or useful
grief.

Consider the vacuum. Five of the protagonists are a
blocked writer, a writer who sells out, a jazz-drummer,
a blues-singer and an actor. Yet it is not a book about
the artist's life and *métier,* nor about creative life. We do
not know what the honest writer in this book is struggling

to say, nor how the other writer has been deceitful, nor what the drummer drums. One tiny bit each is described of the singing and acting, and the gist is significantly how to strike immediately to reality without training and despite a foolish script. There is some too tolerant treatment of Madison Avenue as whorish, but the book is not about this either.

It is puzzling how most of Baldwin's people make a living. One character is a waitress, but nothing more is told; there is once or twice an unspecified hint of a "gig" (or job), but nothing of its pointlessness or exploitation. In two years of sunny love of the actor and a young fellow, it does not once occur to the older man that the youth ought to be making something of himself in the world. The only non-artistic protagonist is a mother, but her motherhood is presented routinely: the author concentrates on her "personal" problem; other couples are explicitly going to be childless. Nobody even mentions any political action or concerted protest, or reasons about the causes and possible remedies of the social situation in which all are trapped. One character is said to be religious, but nothing follows from it in her behavior.

This is not much reality with which to reconstruct the dense world of a serious novel. There is no doubt that this tenuous kind of involvement is in fact the daily experience of millions of people in our society, and they ought to have their Homer. But to make them live, a writer would have to concentrate precisely on their lack of involvement— not on how they "make the scene," but on the important world they fail to make, on their goofing off.

Works like this therefore have a factitious texture. As in prestigious Italian movies or cigarette ads that show the package in front of the landscape, the stars move in front of the scenery of the city, and we are supposed to be interested in their sentiments and interpersonal relations. But they are not *in* the city; they do not influence it, whether powerfully or humbly; they do not rebel against it, so there is no clash; it does not directly crush them, for they are preserved intact in their conceited isolation and illusions about themselves. So their story is not dramatic or terrible. Unless one "identifies" with them (I never do), they are finally otiose.

These novels are a spurious genre. What the writer feels and dreams and somewhat knows is nailed on a wooden framework of narrative, though he is not really story-telling, and the whole is embedded in a cement of documentary background, to make like the world of a novel. In my opinion, these structures are produced only because there is a climate of publishing—for a bad (and big) audience —that demands these "identification" yarns. I doubt that a writer like James Baldwin would go through this song and dance if he followed his best impulse. At his best his prose is very personal, sinuous yet definite, with a slight Negro accent, spare, and very sweet. But in a performance like this it is strained, sometimes journalistic or noisy, often in no idiom, and there are pages of dull conversation and filler. The finest passages, for instance the gentle Marijuana session, are really independent episodes in which he can move freely.

I am judging by a high standard, but otherwise why bother? In the nature of the case, more serious books get more serious criticism; my guess is that *Another Country* has more substance than most books that receive highly respectful reviews. It is mediocre. It is unworthy of its author's lovely abilities. Given his awareness (which he cannot escape), he must write something more poetic and surprising.

•

[*The Design Committee of the American Institute of Architects called together a "First Conference on Aesthetic Responsibility" at the Hotel Plaza in New York, on April 3, 1962.*

During the morning session, I became restive at the streamlined and empty proceedings. At the question period, I asked some trouble-making questions of Mr. Wolfson, the promoter of the new Pan-Am building at Grand Central, a design not generally regarded with favor by the architects at the Conference; and of Mr. Moynihan, a gentleman from the office in charge of Federal building.

Partly, I think, because of my tone, my position in the afternoon's program was shifted from the wind-up speaker, to which I had been assigned, to the first speaker, perhaps to have me over with. Anyway, the following is an edited tape of my remarks. They did not meet with enthusiasm.]

At these meetings I always feel like Banquo's ghost. You have to have him at a banquet, so here I am.

Our theme is: Who is Responsible for Ugliness? I guess we're responsible for ugliness and our hosts here, The American Institute of Architects, are most responsible for ugliness.

I have here a letter from them that I'll read from: "As you can see by the plan of the day, our timing is critical. We feel that a strict observance of the ten minute limit is essential for the pace of the conference as well as to divide time equally among all of the speakers." That is, the time is cut up like bolts of cloth exactly the way Mr. Wolfson over there this morning, cuts up the space to sell it. Now, we don't sell anything here. We *have* all the speakers. And all the speakers means a lot of speakers because, as in any society like ours, we're very greedy, the way Mr. Wolfson is. So we've got to get all the speakers and administer them as tightly as possible.

In these circumstances, apparently, some thought or beauty or intelligence is supposed to occur. It's quite impossible.

Let me go back to the letter. The previous paragraph says, "We look forward to receiving an advance copy of your talk," (that was reasonable, but not from a writer) "to be made available to the press." Obviously public relations are very important. Mr. Moynihan today said that we can now have modern architecture because it's acceptable as the corporate image of the Rockefellers, etc. Therefore it would be acceptable to Jack Kennedy who also is very interested in corporate image.

Under those circumstances, apparently, we're supposed to look to making something beautiful. It is out of the question.

Now, this is supposed to be a conference. But it can't be a conference because under these circumstances there's no thought or talk or real exchange.

What is the meaning of the word "aesthetics" as I heard it all morning and as it exists in the design of this conference? It is something which we tag on and pay attention to as one of the important values. You get the impression that the people who planned this conference had never whittled a spoon or done a stroke of art work in their life. They have a completely unrealistic attitude about how any artist operates. I'm an artist myself; I know. You operate in an art by being interested in something which is worthwhile. You can't be interested in making money for somebody, because that isn't interesting. You have to be interested in some product. Profits are not products. But trade is interesting; to distribute goods, and see people better off. Trade could be very interesting.

Schools are interesting because education is interesting. Housing could be interesting. You have to be interested in some real utility. Our society, however, is not interested in real utility. Therefore it's impossible that anything lovely should be produced.

When an artist is interested in something—I'm interested in some thought I have, or some tree I see—then he gives his feelings to it. Now, what is it to give feelings? One condition is that there has to be a certain amount of sexual freedom, there has to be sexual give, there has to be sexual liberation. I doubt if on this entire panel, from the beginning to the end, the word sex will be mentioned except by me. Yet, apart from it, it's impossible to discuss ugliness and beauty, as everybody knows. For these involve animal qualities of the sensitive soul.

Likewise, there has to be fraternity, someone to give feelings *to*. You have to have some affection for the other people. You have to feel a fraternal give, to want to give. In our city, as we have it, with its segregation, with its one-upping, there is no fraternity. In the country at present, according to the new figures of Mike Harrington which I think were a little low, we have 25% to 30% of people living still in abject poverty. This, at a time when the corporate images of Rockefeller and the rest loom large, and when the government is spending 70% of the national budget on war hardware. Certainly there is no fraternity, there will not be fraternity. Therefore there will be no giving of feeling and no feeling.

In short, there being no interest because there are no real objects to be interested in, there being no real feeling because of our mores, and no true communication because of the lack of fraternity, it is completely unrealistic to have this discussion.

The discussion, though, has to go on because we now have to patch together and make nice a social situation which is not nice. This is a genuine pseudo-event. It should be wiped off the slate, as Veblen would have said.

•

[Review for *Dissent,* Summer, 1960.]

THE ECLIPSE OF COMMUNITY, by Maurice R. Stein. (Princeton University Press)

The Eclipse of Community is a reasoned manual of important American community studies of the past fifty years. One of its great merits is how it implicitly tells the history of half a century by paraphrasing what the successive sociologists have tended to emphasize—from the urban dislocation in the Chicago studies, through the industrial and class conflicts of Middletown and Yankee City, to the suburbanism of Park Forest and Crestwood Heights. As new problems emerge, older ones are paid less attention; but the older ones were not really solved, so there is a deepening crisis; and I guess this is what Professor Stein means by his title.

The book is always interesting and informative, and often lovely. Then reading it, and especially finishing reading it, I am at a loss how (it seems to me) sociology *makes itself* stupid, by the limitations it sets to its inquiry. It is not that the sociologists try to be "scientific" and avoid evaluation. On the contrary, Professor Stein not only probes but evaluates—the criteria are not always explicit —class relations, production and consumption attitudes, conformity and deviation, gaps in the rites of growing up, unconscious alienations and identifications. Yet he austerely will not talk about justice, the value of any of the products or of the culture, the happiness or virtue of any of the people, or the success and failure or effort and struggle of a society in nature and history. There is a good deal of discussion of Identity in this book, but not much mention of the mission, task, justification, or achievement that could constitute an identity. Why must this be? I am puzzled and would like to know, and I am jotting down the following random comments just in order to elicit a reply from the author. For I am convinced that Maurice Stein understands quite well what bothers some of us with present-day sociology, and perhaps he can help us dig what sociologists are doing.

A ludicrous instance: in analyzing the anxiety of suburban women in a commodity-centered society, he says, "Unfortunately the accumulation of appliances can never render cooking permanently meaningful as long as the woman is unsure of its relation to her feminine identity." This is certainly true; but what is (to me) astounding is that nowhere in the discussion does he mention food, feeding a family, the art of cooking, or anything like that, although surely these are the things that must finally make cooking meaningful. Omitting them, how is the cook's identity ever to be realized? What is the merely formal "identity" of a person? Drawing—much too heavily—on Erik Erikson, he says, "Ego-identity depends on the accessibility of roles in which acceptance by significant others is assured. . . . But when the others have begun to question their own identities, (the result is) compulsive role-playing." Certainly; but it does not help a merely formal symbol to multiply it in a hall of mirrors. For a person to *be* somebody—or for there to be a social change or the therapy of a neurosis—at some point there must be real tasks and real achievements. "Being committed" requires more than "meeting expectations"; it requires absorption in some object and world.

The sociologist apparently wants to say that without acceptance and self-acceptance, there cannot be good eating, achieved sex, new science and art, and so forth. Agreed; there cannot. But it is also true that good eating and spontaneous sex, original and disinterested thought, and so forth, are the things that materially constitute acceptance: they make one indispensable, they confirm one's self-appointment, they give courage and security, they *are* identity. In a recent essay on jobs, I argued that the workman's clinging to security comes from the facts that he does not use his particular capacities, and that the product is socially useless; therefore he is not fulfilled and proud, and he is not indispensable. Why do the sociologists *never* mention this kind of proposition? I ask it candidly. Are not achieved real goods, or the failures to achieve real goods, causally operative? Demonstrably and even experimentally? For some reason that I cannot fathom, *these* evaluations are eschewed by sociologists, although they do not avoid evaluating the social structures themselves, in terms of isolation, conflict, insecurity, fragmentation of the process of growing up, *anomie*.

Another aspect of the same is the austere eschewing of underlying "natural" needs and powers as discussable factors, whether by "natural" we mean instinctual, or belonging to the human condition generally, or even culturally ingrained to a degree that they must persist through the arc of change in question. E.g. the appetites, virtues, vices, faculties, that an investigator has to take for granted. For instance, frequently in this book the factor of justice pops up, in speaking of the South, of the Army, and so forth. This is called by Stein "The social-psychological conception of relative deprivation!" Now *is* this adequate to the meaning and *causal power* of justice? He apparently thinks so, for he draws heavily for illustration on the vulgar griping of Bill Mauldin; whereas (it seems to me) the real sociological problem is why there is, in Armies, the childish response of resentment rather than manly indignation and revolt. To answer the real question, we would have to begin at least with Freud's notion of the charismatic father-leader in mass-psychology. And soon we would have to go on to the more important problem of why human beings are so imprudent as to take part in modern war.

Our sociologist mentions this as follows: "The continuous griping about officers and caste deflected attention from more fundamental sources of dissatisfaction potentially arising from the lack of ideological conviction!" (What a beautifully Veblenesque formulation, as if the student were going to go home and tell his father that teacher was a Red, and it was necessary to veil the idea in as thick a smokescreen as possible.) But is this proposition a believable explanation of the lack of war-resisters, of the paralysis of will and reason? Professor Stein cheerily says that "most of us" were in the armed forces, as though it were a matter clear as day; whereas to me it is far more obscure than the doings of Marduk or Tiamat. Without exploring stronger causes, is it possible to cast much light on the Army as a community?

In this study, Urbanization, Industrialization, and Bureaucratization are the contexts of the eclipse of community. They provide an adequate framework to bring us from discussions of the loneliness, ethnical strife, and delinquency of the twenties to the Organized affluence of our suburbs and exurbs (though there curiously remains plenty of loneliness, ethnical strife, and delinquency; I think that the author underestimates the *accumulation* of unsolved problems). What I should like to point out here, however, is how through these changes a kind of "nature" seems to survive, almost like a return of the repressed, and pathetically displaced like any dream symbols. The narrowest rural and small-town family mores *revive* in college towns like Berkeley; handicraft and mechanical skill come back comically as Do It Yourself; and the need for simple loyalty is travestied in being a Company Man. In suburbs, these survivals are trivial; but they are very significant in understanding the theory of Bohemias and some radical groups, which Stein treats inadequately. He lays all his stress on Bohemia as "deviant," and he rightly approves of it as such, as a community laboratory for "innovations"; (though when he seems to imply that therefore we ought to *invent* Bohemias, one does not know whether to laugh or cry: it is just what *Time* and *Life* have been doing for the Beats). But again, what Stein omits is the other side: that a Bohemia at its best is profoundly conservative of nature, insisting on humanly meaningful work, progressive education, better community and sex, *not* because these are innovations, but because they are necessities; just as anarchists are traditional because they think that sun, space, and mutual aid are more basic than economic and social progress. The sociological diagnosis of approvable deviation is a sound and indispensable one; but we must see also the side of stubborn resistance to alienation and *anomie;* otherwise it is inexplicable how a Bohemia could ever produce *worthwhile* innovations, for nothing comes from nothing. (My guess is that our present author is embarrassed in handling these topics, and in handling objective values in general, by restricting himself to formal "community studies," rather than drawing on the more concrete and causal analyses in the poets and novelists. His trouble is analogous to Riesman's naïve notion of defining the "autonomous" man by a poll.)

The eclipse concludes with three chapters that explain the contributions made to community theory by anthropology, psychoanalysis, and sociology. Surely some chapters are missing: Ethics, Theology, Criticism, Political Science. Let me quote two passages. "We have the result—of alienation and anomie—which transforms the human being into an object." If he restricts his methods to anthropology, psychology, and sociology, is he not himself making human society into an object, whose harmonious working would be an end in itself, apart from nature, history, God, or objective value? And does he think that such harmonious working could *indeed* be achieved by devices of anthropology, psychoanalysis, and sociology, without politics, etc.? Again, speaking of a recent study of a community whose motivations are unconscious, he says, " 'Urban dominance' would not be diminished if its existence were known, any more than familiarity with the 'rat race' helps the exurbanites to extract themselves from it." As a pragmatist, I find this an amazing proposition. Are we to call such familiarity *knowledge?* What would be an insight into unconscious motives that did not alter character? And what on earth is the meaning of a truth that does not make a difference in practice?

To repeat, I am convinced that everything I have said here is perfectly familiar to Professor Stein; but I am not familiar with what he would reply. I wish he would tell us.

•

[*In* Dissent, *Summer, 1958.*]

REFLECTIONS ON LITERATURE AS A MINOR ART

I am setting down the following melancholy reflections not with any hope of a remedy, but because the matter is important and nobody else seems to be saying it.

In many ways literature has, in this century, become a minor art, more important than pottery or weaving, perhaps less important than block-printing or other graphics. Firstly, it is no longer an art of either the mass-audience or an élite audience. Cinema and radio-television, journalistic photography and series of illustrations, and persistently architecture and a kind of music: these are arts of the great public in a way that books, even best-sellers, have ceased to be. For the élite, the policy-making, audience, there is no particular art as such; in its artistic taste and needs this group does not distinguish itself from the rest of the people. (To be sure, rich people collect *objects* of painting and sculpture and thereby support artists, but these artists do not produce their works for the collectors any more than poets write for them.)

To the extent that in metropolitan centers the stage is still a popular art, it is not a literary stage, the emphasis being rather on the stars, the spectacle and music, and the production.

The diminution of letters is especially evident to those of us who write very seriously, who try for the classical literary functions of subtile ideas and accurate distinctions, ingenious and cogent reasoning, distilled learning, poetic expression. These functions are not easily or often adapted to the major modern media, to cinema, photography, or television, for in the adaptation they are blurred, blunted, curtailed, and lost. We are not then deceived, like other writers, by the illusion of finding ourselves in the swim; we cannot be made use of; we practice a minor art and occupy a minor place. The comparison to pottery and weaving is apt, for what we are doing is analogous to in-dividual handicraft, no doubt rare and beautiful, com-pared to the major media of the present which tend to be produced by teams with a standard technique, not unlike machine-production.

These are, I suppose, the first decades in the western tradition that letters have not been a major art. It is a situation so peculiar that it is not noticed. Now the shift to other media is not necessarily a cultural misfortune. It happens that, on the whole, cinema and television, etc. have so far produced pathetically inferior works that cannot pretend to compare with the masterpieces of book and stage over 2500 years; but it is not inconceivable that the new media will get hold of themselves (I do not say "mature" since, in cinema at least, the works of a generation ago were much more promising than those today). Naturally, for men of letters our new status is personally unfortunate. We were trained in a tradition where letters had a quite different ambition and scope; our adolescent fantasies of becoming major artists are doomed to be fantasies; and ironically, just because we are too good for the current scene—for we draw on a tradition better than the current scene, but that tradition is irrelevant—we find it hard to adjust to the realities. Also, when, as often, we are called on to teach our English and our Literature, we find ourselves like curators in a museum; the average student (like the average editor and publisher) no longer reads English like a native. This is lonely-making. But as Trotsky said, "History fells the dead wood and the chips fly off."

2

A second way in which literature has diminished is that it is no longer the source of ideas important for social policy and moral behavior. Such ideas as now get influentially abroad—I am not often impressed by their wisdom or brilliance—originate among economists, social scientists, administrators and businessmen, and technologists. Now this lapse of letters from a major position is not a new thing. When Shelley spoke of poets as "unacknowledged legislators," he should have meant not merely that they were unofficial but also, by his time, unaccepted. By the 19th century, compared to the preceding 500 years, although men of letters still had respectable positions in the homes and palaces of the policy-making élite, they certainly had ceased to function as important first sources of ideas that would eventually shape practice. The exceptions stand out and illustrate my point: the social-revolutionary ideas of the Russian writers that brought nearly every major Russian man of letters to jail or exile, or the moral ideas of the European and American writers that at once awakened the censorship. These writers were thinking up ideas not for the makers of policy, but against the makers of policy.

(In general, through the ages we can estimate the importance of letters as sources of policy by the negative test of the censorship of letters. Where books are heavily censored, books are important for social policy and moral behavior; and throughout the high middle ages and in modern times there was always a heavy censorship. But through the 19th century, except in Russia, this decreased, and in our own days it is trivial. Of course in America it is not from the government that we would expect the important censorship of ideas or expression, but from those who control the capital-means of communication, the owners of radio stations, publishers, theatrical producers. Let me then suggest the following possibility: since what these persons do diffuse is not important, policy-making literature, if there exists any important literature at all, it must be in what they refuse to diffuse, what they censor. It is possible that that exists. Note that in our times the question of the *quantity* of diffusion of ideas is essential. Since there is little legal censorship, it is possible for nearly any idea to get itself printed; but our country is swamped with printed matter—more than twenty books a day are printed in large editions and literally tons of newsprint and magazines—and there is no difficulty in muffling any idea at all by refusing to spread it widely. Indeed, we have the interesting paradox of precisely the overworking of printing-presses being a possible cause of the reduction of literature to a minor art.)

So far as the subtile, learned, reasoned, and persuasive treatment of ideas is a function of letters, our present shift to other major media, and literature becoming a minor art, *are* socially unfortunate. Cinematic and pictorial arts do not treat ideas adequately; that is a verbal business, it it specifically literary. Moving pictures can powerfully determine norms of behavior and style of life. The picture-coverage of an event in an illustrated magazine can powerfully direct what people feel about it. But subtle and learned explanation, the application of history and experience, the play of thought and hypothesis, the effort toward the truth under the surface that does not leap to the eye, everything that Matthew Arnold meant by "criticism of life," these things are not skillfully accomplished without letters and training in letters and a high expectation from letters. In the earlier and hotter days of thought, Socrates complained that a book was a poor thing compared to a man because you couldn't question it and reason with it; he would have taken a dim view of audio-visual education.

3

In one important respect, however, literature cannot become a minor art, for it is the art of language. In every generation, the art of letters renovates and codifies the style of speech, assimilating what has sprung up new, inventing new things itself. This is far-reaching, for the style of speech is our interpersonal attitudes, which are largely patterns of rhetoric and syntax; and also the style of speech is a good part of our philosophy of life, for a point of view proves itself viable and gets abroad by being able to tell a real story in a new way. (So the plastic arts, drawing and painting and sculpture, cannot become minor arts for they demonstrate perception, how people can see and are to see; and so a people's music is its kind of feelings.)

Speech is not going to stop changing, and so men of letters, marking down the speech, relating it to character, and developing the characters, are always indispensable. And the strong and subtle writers are fulfilling this function as always. But the mass of speakers are faced with the dilemma: on one horn they must get their style from the writers; on the other they have ceased to follow writing, or expose themselves to it, as major artistic experience. The result is that the ever-new speech is not strongly characterized and explored into its poetry and ideas and assimilated with a great humane tradition; people get their speech, in low-grade letters, as a caricature and a stereotype, with the conformism and small talk or argot that we hear.